Charles Franklin Dunbar

Chapters on Banking

Charles Franklin Dunbar

Chapters on Banking

ISBN/EAN: 9783743313644

Manufactured in Europe, USA, Canada, Australia, Japa

Cover: Foto ©Suzi / pixelio.de

Manufactured and distributed by brebook publishing software (www.brebook.com)

Charles Franklin Dunbar

Chapters on Banking

CHAPTERS

ON

BANKING.

BY
CHARLES F. DUNBAR.

CAMBRIDGE:
1885.

PREFATORY NOTE.

Of the eight chapters here published, the first four were written three years ago, and have been used since as the basis of a short course of lectures on banking, given annually to classes in the elements of political economy. These chapters are now printed, with a slight revision, in the belief that they can be made to answer their purpose best in this form.

The four chapters describing the national banking system of the United States and the banks of England, France, and Germany, were written and are now added to the others, partly for illustration of the general theory of banking and partly to give to the student in convenient form a certain body of information likely to be of use.

CHAPTERS ON BANKING.

CHAPTER I.

DISCOUNT, DEPOSIT AND ISSUE.

1. A BANK may be described in general terms as an establishment, which makes to individuals such advances of the means of payment as may be required and safely made, and to which individuals entrust money, or the means of payment, when not required by them for direct use. In other words, the business of a bank is said to be to lend or discount, and to hold deposits. To these two functions is often added a third, that of issuing banknotes, or the bank's own promises to pay, for use in general circulation as a substitute for money.

The object of the present chapter is to inquire into the real nature of the operations thus roughly classified and usually described by the terms Discount, Deposit, and Issue; and for this purpose we shall analyze the transactions attending the ordinary and simple case of a loan made by a bank to one of its customers.

2. The borrower who procures a loan from a bank does so in order to provide himself with the means, either of making some purchase, or of paying some debt. He seeks, therefore, to obtain, not necessarily money, but a certain amount of purchasing power in some available form, or of whatever may be the usual solvent of debt, measured in terms of money. If we suppose him to be a merchant, buying and selling goods upon credit in the regular course of his business, he is likely at any given time to have in his hands a greater or less number of notes, not yet due, signed by the purchasers to whom he has

heretofore made sales; and it is by a loan upon the basis of one or more of these notes, giving him immediate command of a payment due to him in the future, that he will procure from a bank what he needs. This loan will probably take the form of what is termed a discount. The rate at which the discount shall be made having been settled by agreement, the borrower is entitled to receive from the bank, in exchange for a note due at a future time, the amount promised in the note, less the interest on that amount computed at the agreed rate for the time which the note has still to run.*

The note itself becomes then the property of the bank, to which the promisor is henceforward bound to make the payment at maturity, and the payment thus made restores to the bank the amount advanced by it in exchange for the note, together with the interest which was the inducement for making the exchange. It is now clear, however, that the operation which we have described, although spoken of as a loan by the bank to a borrower, is not a loan in fact. The note when given was evidence that its holder owned the right to receive at a fixed date a certain sum of money, and this right the so-called borrower has sold to the bank. Passing over for the present all question as to what he has received in exchange, his cession of property by sale is as distinct and complete as if he had sold a bale of cotton to another merchant, instead of selling to a bank his right to receive money in the

---

* If *e. g.*, the note discounted promises to pay $2,500, has 87 days to run and the agreed rate is 6 per cent., then the interest to be deducted is $36.25 and the proceeds received by the borrower are $2,463.75. But although this process is commonly known as discount, it gives a result somewhat different from that of discount in the strict sense of the term. Real discount consists in finding that sum which, if put on interest for 87 days at 6 per cent. will then amount to $2,500, or, in other words, in finding the present worth of $2,500 due under the conditions stated. As this present worth is $2,464.27, the established practice gives to the lender a slight profit in addition to that afforded by true discount.

DISCOUNT, DEPOSIT AND ISSUE.

future. It is true that in parting with the note he probably endorsed it, and thus bound himself to make good its amount in case the promisor should fail to do so, but he might equally bind himself by some warranty given to the purchaser, when selling any other description of property. The note has ceased to be his and now takes its place among the investments or securities of the bank, although custom may lead to its classification as a "loan or discount." *

The operation which we have here presented in its simplest form may easily change its shape according to circumstances. Thus our merchant, instead of offering for direct "discount" the notes of his customers, may offer his own note for the sum which he wishes to obtain, and attach to it, as security for its payment at maturity, one or more of the notes of his customers. In this case the principal note, his own, becomes the property of the bank, and the right to receive from him at its maturity the sum promised in it is the real object of sale; while the attached notes, formerly given to him for merchandise and now pledged to the bank as collateral security for the performance of his contract, continue to be his property, subject to the right of the bank to be indemnified therefrom in case of his failure. And so, too, the so-called borrower may offer his own note, secured by the pledge of bonds, stocks, or other valuable property, the ownership of which he does not part with, while at the same time, he sells as effectually as in the first case the right to receive from him a certain sum at a fixed date. Indeed, if we consider any of the forms in which a bank may make "advances" or "loans," we shall find that in every case a right to demand and receive a certain sum of money has been acquired by the bank for a consideration, and that the transaction was, therefore, an exchange.

---

* In an account of the Bank of England, the note supposed, if taken, would have to be classified under "Other Securities," together with bonds or stocks owned by the Bank.

3. We now have to consider what it is that the bank gives in exchange for the right to demand and receive money at a future time, acquired by it under these circumstances. To return to our first and simplest case of so-called discount; the proceeds of the note, or its nominal amount less the interest for the time for which it is to run, are in the first instance placed to the credit of the merchant, to be drawn out by him at once or at different times, as convenience or necessity may dictate. In thus crediting him with the proceeds, the bank plainly gives to him simply the right to call upon it at pleasure for that sum of money. Whether this right is exercised at once by demanding and receiving the money, or whether the exercise of it is postponed as regards the whole or a part of the amount, in either case the right to demand, or to "draw," is the equivalent received by the merchant in exchange for the right sold by him to the bank, of which the note discounted was the evidence. And the sum which he is thus at any time entitled to call for, so long as it stands to his credit, is said to be deposited in the bank, or briefly to be a deposit, standing in his name. So, too, in other cases of so-called "loans" or "discounts," in whatever form and whatever the collateral security held by the bank may be; the operation is always essentially an exchange of rights, whereby the bank acquires the right to receive money, or the legal tender of the country, at some future time, and the individual acquires the right to call for money or legal tender at pleasure. The result is to give the latter that immediate command of purchasing power or of the solvent for debt which, as we have said, is the real object sought by him; but this result is secured at the outset and the relations of the bank and the "borrower" are settled without the intervention of money, by the sale of one right for another.

But the deposit may owe its origin to a different operation from that which has just been examined. It happens every day that the merchant, having cash in hand, sees fit not to hold it in his possession until it is required for use, but prefers to "deposit" it with the bank where he usually transacts his business, until he needs to use it. In this case, when he makes his deposit, the property in the money or substitutes for money actually paid in by him passes to the bank and he receives in exchange the right to demand and receive at pleasure, not that which he paid in, but an equivalent amount.* Here then, as in the former case, the transaction is in effect a sale, although the use of the word "deposit" seems at first to justify an entirely different idea of its character.

4. The other leading operations of banks when analyzed, can also be resolved into cases of the exchange of rights against rights, or of rights against money. As, for example, when the bank, for the convenience of its customer or depositor, undertakes to collect a note due to him by some third party and, the promisor having paid in the amount in money to the bank, it is passed to the credit of the promisee as a deposit. Here the bank has received money for the account of the depositor, and has given to him in exchange a right to draw at pleasure for the amount or any part thereof, the property in the money actually paid having passed absolutely to the bank in exchange for the right to draw. And again, when the bank buys from a merchant a bill of exchange, or when it sells a bill of exchange drawn by itself on some correspondent, it effects an exchange of money against a right, or of a right against money, strongly resembling those already considered. And so, too, if in any of these cases any substitute or equivalent for money is used, instead of money itself, the transaction is still an

---

* It is true that money may be left as a "special deposit" with a bank, just as plate, jewels, or other valuables may be, in which case, the identical money deposited is to be returned and the bank consequently does not acquire the property in the thing deposited, but is merely entrusted with its temporary custody. This, however, is not a banking operation, and the deposit in this case is made with the bank, not because it is a bank, but because it owns a strong vault.

exchange of a right on the one side, and some means of payment on the other, the latter becoming the property of the bank.

We have thus far, for the sake of simplicity, spoken only of the "rights to receive" money, bought by the bank in one class of cases, and sold by it in another. But where there is a right to receive on the part of the creditor, there is a corresponding duty to pay on the part of the debtor; and these rights or credits, when viewed from the other side, are, therefore, debts or liabilities. It follows then that, as any addition to the loans of a bank is an increase of its investments or resources, so any addition to its deposits is an increase of its debts or liabilities. The deposit which is credited in making a loan is a liability to pay on demand, assumed by the bank in exchange for a security promising a payment to the bank in the future; and the deposit credited upon the receipt of cash from the depositor is a similar liability, assumed in exchange for so much money or so much of its substitutes.

5. A little consideration of the manner in which notes are issued by banks will show that in the banknote we have only another form of liability, differing in appearance but not in substance, from the liability for deposits. The banknote is the duly certified promise of the bank to pay on demand, adapted for convenient circulation as a substitute for the money which it promises. It is issued, by the bank, and can be issued, only to such persons as are willing to receive the engagement of the bank in this form instead of receiving money, or instead of being credited with a deposit. Thus the so-called borrower, who in the first instance has been credited with a deposit and to whom the bank is therefore to this extent liable, may prefer to draw the amount in notes of the bank and to use them in making his payments. But, in this case, it is plain the liability of the bank is changed only in form; it is still a liability to pay a certain sum of money on demand. And so if the depositor deposits money and receives notes, or receives notes in satisfaction of a demand of any kind against the bank,

he, in fact, foregoes the use of the money itself and consents to receive in its stead a promise to pay upon demand, and to receive the evidence of that promise in the form of notes rather than in another. The question, in which form he shall hold his right of demand against the bank, is one to be decided by the nature of his business or by his present convenience, but plainly the decision of the question in no way affects the relation between himself or any transferee of his right and the bank. The notes issued by a bank are thus a liability distinguishable in form only from its liability for deposits.

6. In the operations which have now been considered the subject-matter involved is in every case either money or contracts for the payment thereof. No form of dealing in merchandize or real property comes properly within the province of banking. And, inasmuch as a contract for the payment of money may be viewed either as a credit or as a debt, according as it is looked at from the one side or the other, banking is sometimes described as the business of dealing in credits and sometimes as that of dealing in debts. For the transaction of this business in the modern world both of the functions "discount" and "deposit" are indispensable. In order to be a bank, that is to say, an establishment must carry on the purchase of rights to demand money in the future, or securities; and it must also use in some form or other its own engagements for the payment of money upon demand.* If it practices the former only, it is simply an investor of its own money, as any private individual may be; if it practises the latter only, it may indeed be said to be a bank of the obsolete type of the Bank of Amsterdam, but it would then cease to answer the chief purpose of a bank of the present age, viz., that of enabling individuals to convert into immediate purchasing power the debts which are due to them in the future.

---

* See in Bagehot's *Lombard Street*, p. 212, a remark that the Rothschilds are great capitalists, but are not bankers.

The use of the third function, however, that of issue, is not indispensable to the existence of a bank, for, as has been shown, issue is but a modification of deposit, and is made for convenience and not from necessity. There are conditions under which the liability of the bank in the form of notes is desired for use, and there are also conditions under which the liability in the form of deposits better serves the convenience of individuals or of the community. Many banks, therefore, carry on a large and successful business without making any issue of notes whatever.*

It must be added that incorporation by law is not a necessary condition of the existence of a bank.† Discount and deposit, and if no legal prohibition exists, issue also, may be carried on by individuals and firms as well as by incorporated companies. It is true that in discussions of banking it is usual to give almost exclusive attention to incorporated banks, partly because they usually hold a more conspicuous position and partly because their affairs are in some degree open to official inspection, so that the details of their business are known, at least in part, whereas the transactions of private banks are known only to the persons concerned. It is none the less true, however, that in the economic effects of their transactions the two kinds of banks do not differ, and that neither can be neglected in an examination of the economic problems presented by any community in which it is found to exist.

---

* In November, 1882, the banks in operation in the United States, excluding savings banks, were classified as follows:—

	Number.	Capital.
State Banks and Trust Companies,	1,061	$123.1 millions.
Private Bankers	3,412	105.3 "
National Banks	2,308	484.9 "
Total	6,781	$713.3 "

See Comptroller's Report, 1884, p. 8. Of these banks the national banks alone are authorized by law to issue notes.

† See the preceding note.

CHAPTER II.

BANKING OPERATIONS AND ACCOUNTS.

1. HAVING thus taken a general view of the nature of banking operations, it is now necessary that we should enter upon the consideration of some of their details.

For a bank, as well as for any other considerable establishment, it is requisite that a capital should be provided at the outset. There can be no constant proportion between the amount of this capital and the extent of the business which may be built up by its means. We can only say that, other things being equal, the larger the business that can be carried on with safety with a given capital, the larger will be the field from which profits can be earned and the higher the proportion which the profits will bear to the original outlay; but the point at which the extension of the business passes the line of safety, must be determined by the circumstances of the particular bank, by the kind of business carried on by those dealing with it, and by the condition of the community in which it is established. The attempt has sometimes been made to limit by law for incorporated banks the proportion of transactions for a given amount of capital,* but no such provision has any foundation except a conjectured average, too rough to be of service in any individual case. In this respect, as in so many others, the judgment of the persons most interested, acting under the law of self-preservation, is far more trustworthy than any legislative decision.

The capital thus to be provided at the outset is, of course, in

---

**E. g.*, the law in Massachusetts formerly limited loans to double the amount of the capital. See *Revised Statutes of 1860*, c. 57, § 25.

the case of a private bank, the contribution of the partners, as in any other undertaking. In the case of an incorporated bank the capital is divided by law into equal shares or units of fixed amount, as *e. g.*, under the law of the United States, a capital of $100,000 into 1,000 shares of $100 each; and of these shares the individual shareholders contribute in such proportion as they please. The law may as a matter of public policy limit the proportion of capital stock to be owned by any one individual or firm, and it may also limit the liability of shareholders for debts due by the bank, in case of its failure; but, it may be said in general that in the absence of special provisions to the contrary, the powers, rights and liabilities of each shareholder are now usually determined by the number of shares of the stock contributed or owned by him. In the election of directors and of other officers for the immediate management of the business, each share usually entitles its owner to cast one vote; the dividend of profit is divided in the ratio of shares owned, and contributions to meet losses, if required by law, are called for in the same ratio.

The capital which has been subscribed by the intending shareholders must necessarily be paid in in money or in the legal tender of the country. It is not necessary that the whole should be paid in at the outset, but the payment of the whole usually precedes the full establishment of the business; and, in the case of incorporated banks, the law is apt to require that some definite proportion, as *e. g.*, one-half, shall be paid in before the opening of business, in order to insure good faith and a solid basis for the business undertaken.*

---

* The English Joint Stock Banks present some remarkable cases of partially paid capital. Thus the largest, the London and Westminster, has £20 in the £100 paid up on its shares, and the London Joint Stock has £15. In these cases, the business having been fully established by means of a part only of the nominal capital, the liability of the shareholders to contribute the remainder in case of need constitutes a species of guaranty fund of immense amount.

BANKING OPERATIONS AND ACCOUNTS. 15

If, now, we undertake to represent by a brief statement of account the condition of a bank having a capital of $100,000 paid in, on the morning when it opens its doors for business, we shall have the following:

Liabilities.	*Resources.*
Capital . . . $100,000.	Specie . . . $100,000.

It may at first sight appear to be a contradiction in terms, that the capital should be set down as a liability and not as a resource. But we must here distinguish between the financial liability for what has been received from the shareholders and the right of property in the thing received. The bank has become accountable to its shareholders for the amounts paid in by them respectively, but the money actually paid has become the property of the bank; or, in the language of accountants, the bank has become *liable* for its capital, and the money in hand is for the present its *resource* for meeting this liability, or for explaining the disposition made of what has been received.

As the bank requires banking rooms and a certain supply of furniture and fixtures for the convenient transaction of its business, we may suppose it to expend $5,000 of its cash in providing this "plant." The property thus procured, with the remaining $95,000 in cash will then be the aggregate resources by means of which the capital is to be accounted for, and the account will stand as follows:

Liabilities.	*Resources.*	
Capital . . . $100,000	Real estate, furniture, fixtures, etc. .	$5,000
	Specie	95,000
$100,000		$100,000

2. The bank, however, cannot answer the purposes of its existence, or earn a profit for its shareholders, until its idle cash is converted into some kind of interest-bearing security. Nor is it enough that a permanent investment of the ordinary kind should be made, as by the simple exchange of its cash for government bonds or railway securities. It is the chief business of the bank to afford to purchasers and dealers the means of using, by anticipation, funds which are receivable by them in the future, and this implies both the purchase of private securities or "business paper" to a considerable extent and also frequent change and renewal of purchases. Moreover, while the private capitalist finds it advantageous to make simple investments of a permanent sort, this would plainly be unprofitable for the shareholders of a bank, who have to pay from its profits some serious expenses of management, and need, therefore, a larger field for earnings than the ordinary returns on their capital alone. The bank is obliged then to use its credit in some way for the extension of its operations. It is in fact, by such a use of its credit, that it becomes in reality a bank.

Most of the conditions of the case are best answered by the "discount" of commercial paper as above described. The time for which such obligations have to run varies with the custom of the trade which gives rise to them, but is in most cases sufficiently short so that the re-payment to the bank is early. And even where custom gives the paper longer time, if the paper itself is used only as a collateral security, the note which is the actual object of negotiation with the bank is by preference usually made not to exceed four months. It is easy then to arrange the purchases of paper with reference to the times of maturity, so as to provide for a steady succession of payments to the bank, and thus facilitate the reduction of the business if necessary, or its direction into new channels, as prudence or good policy may require. The certainty of prompt payment

BANKING OPERATIONS AND DEPOSITS.

at maturity, needed for this end, is presented in a high degree by the paper created in the ordinary course of business. * Independently of the collateral security which the bank may hold, the written promise of the merchant or manufacturer to pay on a fixed day is an engagement which involves the credit of the promisor so far, that failure is an act both of legal insolvency and of commercial dishonor. Selected with judgment then, such paper is not only the investment which most completely answers the purposes of the bank's existence, but is probably as safe as any investment which could be found.

It may easily happen, however, that the bank may find it desirable to invest a part of its resources in some other form, either because good commercial paper cannot be procured in sufficient amount, or as a matter of policy. In this case it will purchase such other securities as offer, not only complete safety of investment, but the possibility of easy conversion into cash in case of need.† In this country United States bonds, and many descriptions of State, municipal and corporation bonds might answer this purpose. Stocks would more rarely answer it, being more liable to the fluctuations in price caused by misfortune or the ordinary vicissitudes of business. Mortgages of real estate, however, would not be admissible, except when held as a security collateral to some other more easily convert-

---

* The reports of a large commercial agency show that, for ten years, 1875–84, the number of failures in the United States was a trifle over one per cent. of the whole number of houses reported as in business. For a curious estimate showing that the liabilities of failed firms in 1874 amounted to less than one-fourth of one per cent. of the total commercial liabilities of the country for the year, see *Commercial and Financial Chronicle*, February, 1875, p. 129.

† See in the reports of the Comptroller of the Currency, the "United States bonds on hand" and "other stocks and bonds" held by the national banks and amounting to over $109,000,000 in July, 1885. Compare also the "government securities" held by the banking department of the Bank of England.

ible, for even when the mortgaged property is so ample and stable as to insure the goodness of the mortgage, the conversion of the mortgage into cash by sale is not always easy, and is especially difficult at those times when the bank most needs to have all its resources at command. Indeed, the danger to be apprehended from the locking up of resources in securities, which may be solid but are not easily realized, is so great, that it has been said to be the first duty of the banker to learn to distinguish between a note and a mortgage, his business lying with the former. Real estate, of course, cannot be regarded as a banking security, however desirable it may be as an investment for individuals, for it is not only subject to great fluctuations in value, but is at times unsaleable; and the law of the United States therefore wisely prohibits investments in it by the national banks, except so far as is necessary for the accommodation of their business.*

The results of the process of investment in commercial paper and in other securities are best understood when we trace the effect in the accounts of the bank. Taking then the account as it stood on p. 15, let us suppose that the bank buys securities from those dealing with it, or in the common phrase, makes "loans to its customers," to the amount of $90,000, the paper being in many pieces and having various lengths of time to run, but averaging three months. Supposing the interest to be computed at six per cent., we should have the account changed by the operation as follows:

Liabilities.		Resources.	
Capital	$100,000	Loans	$90,000
Undivided profits	1,350	Real estate, furniture, fixtures, etc.	5,000
Deposits	88,650	Specie	95,000
	$190,000		$190,000

---

* See *Revised Statutes*, § 5137.

BANKING OPERATIONS AND ACCOUNTS. 19

Here we have the securities which certify the right of the bank to demand and receive $90,000 at a future date placed among the resources; the net proceeds of the securities, or the aggregate of the sums which the bank holds itself liable to pay for them on demand, stand among the liabilities as deposits; and the interest deducted in advance, or the profit on the operation, which the bank must at the proper time account for to its stockholders, also stands as a liability. This, however, is the condition of the account at the moment of making the investment, when the bank has made its purchase of securities by merely creating a liability. As this liability is real and must be met, so far as the depositors who own it see fit to press it, let us suppose that depositors call for cash to the amount of $15,000, and we shall have a further change in the account as follows:

Liabilities.		*Resources.*	
Capital	$100,000	Loans	$90,000
Undivided profits	1,350	Real Estate, etc.	5,000
Deposits	73,650	Specie	80,000
	$175,000		$175,000

It is clear that unless the enforcement of the liability for deposits and consequent withdrawal of specie goes much farther than this, the bank can safely increase its loans or its purchase of securities, although its method of doing so is by the increase of its liabilities. We will suppose it, therefore, to have expanded its affairs until it has reached something like the average condition in November, 1884, of those banks in the United States, which, being incorporated under the laws of the several states, are not authorized to issue notes. It will then stand thus:

Liabilities.		Resources.	
Capital	$100,000	Loans	$299,000
Surplus	28,000	Bonds and stocks	30,000
Undivided profits	11,000	Real estate	13,000
Deposits	294,000	Other assets	15,000
		Expenses	1,000
		Cash items	26,000
		Specie	23,000
		Legal tender notes	26,000
	$433,000		$433,000

3. Postponing for the present the consideration of some terms which here occur for the first time, it appears from the above account that purchases of securities have been made to more than three times the amount of the capital, and that this has been effected chiefly by the creation of liabilities in the form of deposits. What determines the limit to which this process can be carried?

If depositors seldom demanded the payment to which they are entitled, and were contented with the mere transfer of their rights among themselves as a conventional currency, the bank might dispense with holding specie or cash in any form and keep all its resources employed in its productive securities. The expansion of the deposits would then resemble in its effects the expansion of any other currency and might go on until a check should be interposed by the consequent rise of prices and demand for specie for exportation. And it is true, as we shall see, that in communities where banking is largely practised, the use of deposits as currency by transfer from hand to hand is so extensive, that a bank in good credit can rely upon their being withdrawn so slowly, or rather to so small an extent, as to make it unnecessary to have cash in readiness for the payment of more than a small proportion at any given moment. In a period of financial disorder or alarm, withdrawals may be more frequent or more immediate, and a larger provision of cash may be needed for safety, than at other times; the kind of business carried on by depositors may expose one bank, or the banks in one place, to unusually heavy occasional demands, or may on the other hand make demands steadier, than is the case elsewhere; a city bank may be more subject to heavy calls from depositors than a country bank; still, for every bank in its place and under the circumstances of the time there is some line below which its provision of cash, or reserve as it is now called, cannot safely fall. And the necessity of maintaining this minimum reserve fixes a limit to the ability of the bank to increase its securities. For obviously, in the account last given, any increase of securities, that is of loans or bonds, must be effected, either by an increase of deposits, or by an actual expenditure of cash. In the one case the proportion of reserve to demand liabilities would be weakened by the increase of liabilities; in the other it would be weakened by the decrease of cash. If, then, the reserve were already as low as prudence would allow, or were threatened by approaching heavy demands from depositors, no increase of securities could be made without serious risk.

What proportion the reserve should bear to the liabilities which it is to protect is a question which the law has sometimes attempted to settle, by requiring a certain minimum,* leaving it to every individual bank to determine for itself how much is required in addition to this minimum. And this is no doubt as far as any general rule can go. As has already been suggested, the requirements for safety of different banks and of different places must vary, and so must the requirements of the same bank at different times.† It can only be said that

---

* The law of the United States, under which the national banks are established, recognises twenty-five per cent. as the minimum reserve for city banks, and fifteen per cent. as the minimum for country banks. *Revised Statutes*, §5191.

† The Bank of England may be content with a reserve amounting to 33 per cent. of its deposits, as in October, 1885, or it may be uneasy with a reserve amounting to 44 per cent., as in August, 1881.

the reserve should be large enough, not only to insure the imdiate payment of any probable demand from depositors, but also to secure the bank from being brought down to the "danger line" by any such demand. If twenty-five per cent. is the minimum consistent with safety, the reserve should be far enough above this to be secure from reduction to a point where any further demand or accident may make the situation hazardous.*

4. In the arrangement of its reserve the bank itself necessarily feels a strong conflict of interests. On the one hand it is impelled to increase its securities as far as possible, for it is from them that it derives its profits, and the retention of a large amount of idle cash is felt as a loss. On the other hand, the maintenance of a reserve sufficient, not only to continue its payments but to inspire the public with confidence in its ability to do so, is a necessity of its existence, even though a part of its resources do thus appear to be kept permanently idle. As a natural consequence, the actual settlement of the question in favor of a large or of a small reserve in any particular case will depend largely on the temperament of the managers. In every banking community may be found "conservative" banks, the caution of whose managers forbids them to take risks by extending their business at the expense of an ample reserve; and by their side may be seen the more "active" banks, whose managers habitually spread all possible sail, and provide for the storm only when it comes.

It is to be observed that the necessity of providing a cash reserve is not met by the excellence of the securities held by the bank. Although the certainty of payment at maturity be absolute, still the demands upon the bank are demands for cash, and cannot be answered by the offer of even the best securities. If the depositor or creditor does not receive cash in full for

---

* For a discussion of this subject, see Bagehot's *Lombard Street*, ch. xii.

his demand when it is made, the bank has failed, and any satisfaction of his claim by the delivery of a security is, as it were, only the beginning of a division of the property of the bank among its creditors. Specie, or the paper which is a substitute for it as a legal tender for debts, form the only real banking reserve. The reserve of the bank may, however, be greatly strengthened by a judicious arrangement of its securities. For example, if, in the account above given, the "bonds and stocks" are, as they should be, of descriptions which are readily saleable, they afford the means of replenishing the reserve in case of need, without foregoing the enjoyment of an income from this amount of resources for the present. In extreme cases of general financial panic, it is true, even the strongest government securities may find but few purchasers;* still such a provision is the best support which can be had in the absence of, or as an auxiliary to, a sufficient reserve of actual cash.

The natural method of securing the proper apportionment of resources between securities and reserve, under ordinary circumstances, is by increasing or diminishing the loans, or, in other words, the purchases of securities made from day to day in the regular course of business. That part of the securities which consists of the promises of individuals or firms to pay to the bank at fixed dates, is made up of many such pieces of commercial paper, maturing, if properly marshalled, in tolerably regular succession. The payment of one of these engagements when it becomes due may be made either in money, or by the surrender to the bank of an equal amount of its own liabilities, as will be shown in the next chapter. In the former case, the payment of the maturing paper to the bank is in fact the conversion of a security into cash, and increases the reserve without change in the liabilities; in the

---

* In the London market in the panic of May, 1866, there was a moment when even "consols were unsaleable." *Patterson, Science of Finance*, 223.

latter, the reduction of securities is balanced by a reduction of liabilities which raises the proportion of reserve. If, then, the bank stops its "discounts" or the investments in new securities, or if it even slackens its usual activity in making such investments, the regular succession of maturing paper will gradually strengthen its reserve; if it increases its activity in investment, it will lower or weaken its reserve; and if it adjusts the amount of its new investments to the regular stream of payments made by its debtors, it may keep the strength of its reserve unaltered, until some change in the condition of affairs brings cash to it or takes cash away by some other process.

This natural dependence of the reserve upon the more or less rapid reinvestment of its resources by the bank is distinctly recognized by the law of the United States, which provides that when the reserve of any national bank falls below the legal minimum, such bank "shall not increase its liabilities by making any new loans or discounts," until its reserve has been restored to its required proportion.* By a less harsh application of the same principle, the Bank of England operates upon its reserve by lowering or raising its rate of discount and thus encouraging or discouraging applications for loans. And it was with a view of facilitating the replenishment of the reserve by the curtailment of loans, that the law of Louisiana formerly provided that the banks established by that State should hold a considerable proportion of "short bills," or paper maturing within ninety days, so that the constant stream of payments of such paper might always insure the early command of a large part of its resources by the bank.†

5. To return in conclusion to the account given on p. 20; we have there among the liabilities certain sums classified as "surplus" and as "undivided profits." Taken together these

---

* *Revised Statutes of the United States*, § 5191.

† See some remarks on the excellent effects of the Louisiana system by Samuel Hooper, *Theory and Effects of Laws regulating specie in Banks*, 1860.

sums represent profits which have been made, but not divided among the stockholders, and which are therefore to be accounted for by the bank. The surplus is that portion of these profits which as a matter of policy it has been determined not to divide and pay over to the stockholders, but to retain in the business, as in fact, although not in name, an addition to the capital. The remainder, the undivided profits, is the fund from which, after payment of current expenses and of any losses which may occur, the next dividend to the stockholders will be made. The current expenses are for the present entered on the other side of the account, as they represent a certain amount of cash which has disappeared; but at the periodical settlement of accounts they will be deducted from the undivided profits and will thus drop out from the statement. "Other assets," here set down as an investment, is supposed to cover any form of property held by the bank and not otherwise classified, but especially doubtful securities, or such property, not properly dealt in by a bank, as it may have been necessary to take and to hold temporarily, for the purpose of securing some debt not otherwise recoverable. For example, although the bank could not properly invest in a mortgage, it might be wise for it to accept a mortgage in settlement with an embarrassed debtor, and in this case the mortgage would stand among the "other assets." And, finally, "cash items" include such demands on individuals or other banks as are to be collected in cash and are therefore deemed the equivalent of cash in hand. In the absence of any legal provision limiting the treatment of such demands as reserve by the creditor, they may be regarded as virtually a part of the reserve, which in the case before us may therefore be treated as made up of cash items, specie, and legal tender notes.

To illustrate what has been said in this chapter we will now suppose the bank, with its affairs standing as on p. 20, to make the following operations:

a. To add to its securities by discount of three months

paper $20,000, of which three-fourths are purchased by the creation of liabilities, and one-fourth by the expenditure of cash. The account would then stand as follows:

Liabilities.		Resources.	
Capital	$100,000	Loans	$319,000
Surplus	28,000	Bonds and stocks	30,000
Undivided profits	11,300	Real estate	13,000
Deposits	308,775	Other assets	15,000
		Expenses	1,000
		Reserve	70,075
	$448,075		$448,075

b. To retrace its steps by diminishing its "discounts" or holding of securities to the extent of $50,000, of which four-fifths are paid to it by the surrender of demands for deposits to a like amount and one-fifth in cash; to pay $1,250 for current expenses; and further to increase its reserve by the sale of bonds and stocks to the amount of $10,000. The following would then be the state of the account:

Liabilities.		Resources.	
Capital	$100,000	Loans	$269,000
Surplus	28,000	Bonds and stocks	20,000
Undivided profits	11,300	Real estate	13,000
Deposits	268,775	Other assets	15,000
		Expenses	2,250
		Reserve	88,825
	$408,075		$408,075

c. To sell $2,000 of its other assets for cash with a loss of $500; to make a semi-annual dividend of four per cent., of which one-half is credited to stockholders who happen to be depositors also, and one-half is paid in cash; and to carry the remainder of its undivided profits to surplus. The account would then stand at the beginning of the new half year, as follows:

Liabilities.		Resources.	
Capital	$100,000	Loans	$269,000
Surplus	32,550	Bonds and stocks	20,000
Deposit	270,775	Real estate	13,000
		Other assets	13,000
		Reserve	88,325
	$403,325		$403,325

CHAPTER III.

THE CHECK SYSTEM.

1. In the preceding chapter reference has been made more than once to the transfer of deposits by one holder to another, and to their consequent use as currency. It is now necessary to examine more closely the simple machinery by which this transfer is effected. The depositor, or the creditor of the bank, having to make a payment to some other person, has his choice between two methods of making it. He may demand money from the bank, in the exercise of his right as a creditor, and deliver this money; or, with the assent of the person to whom he has to make payment, he may give to this person an order on the bank for the money, or what is commonly called a check. If he adopts the latter method, a payment for goods or of a debt is effected as between the parties, by the simple transfer of a right to demand money from the bank; and so if the recipient of the check gives it in payment to some third person, and he to a fourth, and so on. To this extent the check is plainly made a substitute for the sum of money for which it calls. It represents no particular money in existence, for, as we have seen, the deposit is likely to have been created by the bank in exchange for some security bought by it, and is, therefore, a naked right to demand, and not a claim to any particular cash; and even if the deposit originated in the lodgment of money by the depositor, it has in this case also become a naked right to demand and not a claim to the money actually deposited. But the transfer of this naked right is made by the agreement of the parties to serve the same purpose as the transfer of money, and the right thus becomes a substitute for money.

The effectiveness of this substitution, however, is vastly increased and the use of the deposit prolonged, where it is the practice for the transferee himself to deposit the check, instead of either making a fresh transfer of it or of demanding its payment by the bank.

If we suppose all the parties concerned to keep their accounts with a single bank, and suppose a check for $2,000 to have been drawn by A against his deposit in the bank and given by him to B in payment for goods, B may deposit this check to his credit as he would money. The transfer of the right by A to B has now been made complete, for the bank has become a party to it, and has cancelled its liability for $2,000 to A by recognizing a liability for a like amount to B. This novation, or change of creditors, has not only secured B against the possibility of finding that, before his own check was presented, A's deposit in the bank had been exhausted by other checks drawn fraudulently or by mistake by A, but it has also made B's right of demand against the bank divisible at pleasure, since this has now become a right to draw his own check or checks to an amount not exceeding $2,000 in all. Checks become, therefore, the instruments by which rights to demand money may be transferred from one individual to another in such amounts as the transactions between them may require; and when we consider the great security and convenience of transfer by such means as compared with actual payment in money, there is little need of furthur explanation of the astonishing extent to which they are now used, especially in English-speaking communities.*

---

*It has been found by observation that in New York, at two different dates, 97.7 per cent. of the total receipts of the banks were in checks and similar instruments calling for money at sight. In the United States as a whole the proportion was 94.6 per cent. In London it has been reported as 97.2 per cent. See *Comptroller's Report* for 1881, pp. 13-23 for an important investigation of this subject.

THE CHECK SYSTEM.

If, now, we suppose the parties concerned to keep their accounts with different banks in the same city, we shall have results a little more complex but not different in kind. In this case we may suppose the check drawn by A upon Bank No. 1 to be deposited by B in Bank No. 2. If the transaction stands alone, the latter bank collects the money called for by the check, and holds itself liable to make payment to B on demand in sums to suit his pleasure. Then has there been a change, not only of creditors, but of debtors, and yet at the close, after the payment by A to B has been completed, we have in existence a bank liability of the same amount as that with which we started. Probably, however, in a community where there were several banks, the transaction would not stand alone. At the end of a day's business each bank would be likely to have in its possession, received in deposit, checks upon several, and perhaps all, the others; each would then have checks to meet as well as checks to collect; and in this case each would make its settlement with another, not by making mutual demands and mutual payments, but by the offsetting of demands and the payment only of such balance as might then remain due from the one or the other. If, at the end of the day Bank No. 1 had received in deposit checks upon Bank No. 2 to the amount of $25,000, and Bank No. 2 in like manner, checks upon Bank No. 1 amounting to $23,000, the account as between the banks would be settled easily by the payment of $2,000 by Bank No. 2 to Bank No. 1, while Bank No. 1 would have made itself liable to pay $25,000 to its depositors upon demand, and Bank No. 2 would have become liable to its depositors for $23,000. And the result is the same if the operation here traced is multiplied by the number of banks carrying on business with each other in a great city. The settlement of accounts by the banks with each other still leaves the banks collectively under the same liability for payment on demand as before. The liability rests upon the banks, it may be, in different proportions, and is differently distributed among the creditors; but so long as payments are made by checks and checks deposited, the right to demand from a bank which is called a deposit continues to exist in somebody's possession, and is as well fitted to discharge the office of money as when it was first created.

2. This medium of payment acquires great perfection wherever the Clearing House system is adopted. Under this system a daily meeting takes place, at which all the banks carrying on business at any common centre are represented. Each bank turns in at the central office all the checks and cash demands which it holds against the others and is credited therewith; the checks and demands which have thus been brought together against each are then summed up and charged against it; and the balance found to be due from each bank or to it is then paid to or from the central office in money. By this means a great mass of transactions, which would otherwise require a series of demands by each bank upon every other, are settled at once and the transportation of large sums in cash from one bank to another is to a great extent dispensed with.*

Under this arrangement the bank deposit, circulated by means of checks, becomes the most convenient means of pay-

---

* For a further notice of the Clearing House system, see Note on p. 37. The transportation of cash referred to in the text is reduced to its minimum by the practice sometimes adopted of using "Clearing House certificates" instead of money or legal tender notes. These certificates represent money or notes deposited with the Clearing House, or with some bank which is its representative for this purpose, and are payable on demand; being made in convenient denominations they are used in payments between the banks, and for the purposes of reserve are recognized by the law of the United States as the equivalent of the cash which they represent. *Revised Statutes*, § 5192. The same object is secured in London, where banks and bankers keep their cash balances at the Bank of England, by transfers at that Bank.

THE CHECK SYSTEM. 31

ment yet devised. A stroke of the pen transfers it in whatever amount is needed for the largest transaction, and this transfer instantly becomes the basis for fresh operations, with security against accidental loss as complete as can be imagined. In the strict economic sense this medium, no doubt, has rapidity of circulation in a high degree, while in the sense of actual activity of movement in a given time it far outstrips money or notes, and has been well said to be the most volatile⁽²⁾ of all the mediums of exchange. Of the entire circulating medium of this country it forms incomparably the greatest, although the least considered, part. Depending for its efficiency solely upon convention and issued as well by private firms as by incorporated banks,* it for the most part eludes that regulation which legislatures so industriously enforce upon the other constituents of the currency. Indeed, beyond the requirement of a minimum reserve to be held by incorporated banks, as for example in the United States, we may say that the subject is not touched by legislation. The necessity for payment in specie upon demand, which is the most important safeguard of value, is the result of the general provision for the payment of debts of any kind. And the chief assurance against excessive expansion on the part of any single establishment is given by the certain demand for prompt and frequent settlement, occasioned by the voluntary establishment of the Clearing House, or by the habits of the community, but not by law.

3. What natural limit is to be found then to the continued circulation of a liability for deposit when once it is created and set in motion by the process of "discount?"

Plainly, if at any stage the holder of a check, instead of depositing it, demands its payment in money by the bank on

---

* Of the twenty-seven members of the London Clearing House, twelve are private banking houses. "The joint-stock banks were not admitted until 1854, nor the Bank of England until ten years later." Gilbart, *Principles and Practice of Banking* (edition of 1873), 452.

which it is drawn, the payment to that extent extinguishes the liability. It is quite possible that the money, after a brief circulation, may find its way back, in the deposits of cash made by one or more individuals, and so a new liability similar to the old one may come into existence; but, nevertheless, we may fairly say that the use of the deposit as a substitute for money came to a natural close with the payment of the check. Except, however, in the cases where money is required for some special purpose, as to be sent abroad or to some other part of the country, or for the increase of the stock in the hands of the public, this limit to the circulation of deposits is not of great importance. For, as the withdrawal of specie under ordinary circumstances is merely the exchange of one medium of payment for another, any withdrawal on a large scale would imply such a change in the habits and preferences of the public as is not often or easily made.

A most important limit is found, however, in the use of deposits for the payment of debts due to the bank. That the depositor can, to the extent of his deposit, pay a debt due from himself to the bank by the relinquishment of the bank's debt to him, needs no explanation. In practice he draws his own check in favor of the bank and exchanges it for the obligation held against him by the bank, this mutual release being for each side as effectual a discharge of liability as a payment in money could have been. The payment in this manner of the debt due by the depositor and standing among the securities or loans of the bank, finally cancels a liability of the bank, equal in amount to that which was created when the loan was made.* It matters little by what process the deposit, or right of demand, finally used by the depositor in payment came into his possession. If he is a merchant he has probably collected smaller sums which were due to him, for the purpose of his payment to the bank, and these smaller sums are likely to have

---

* Compare the statement of account for operation *b.* on p. 26.

come to his hands to a great extent in the shape of checks, which, as we have seen, were the instruments for transferring to him the rights of demand which others held against the bank. If he borrowed the means of payment, he in all probability received the amount in a check. Nor is the case different when there are several banks, and the depositor has received his collections in checks drawn upon other banks than his own. As was seen when we were considering the payment by check in § 1, the deposit of these checks to his credit effected a transfer of the liability from the other banks to his own; and here also this liability is finally extinguished when he uses it in payment of his debt to the bank.

It is possible, indeed, that the payment should be made by the debtor to the bank in money, or by a check drawn against a fresh deposit of money, and in this case there is either no extinguishment of bank liability by the payment, or only the new liability created by the fresh deposit is extinguished. But in a community where banking is firmly and widely established, the great payments of commerce and of general business are certain to be made, for the most part, in the medium which is most accessible and most convenient for use in large sums, and this medium is undoubtedly that which is commonly termed bank deposits.

It appears then that deposits are created by the act of the bank, when loans are increased, and that they are cancelled when loans are paid.* There is, therefore, a rough correspondence between the movements of loans and of deposits. This correspondence may be weakened by the actual flow of money to or from the bank, but in the ordinary movements of business it is tolerably close, and where it fails the apparent exception will be found to be explained by some special condition of

---

* For some striking remarks on this subject, see Hamilton's report on a National Bank, *Works*, III. 109.

the case.* It will be found in general that, at times when banks are increasing their operations, their deposits swell, and that when they are contracting, their deposits fall. The true connection between these movements is often forgotten, but its nature cannot be mistaken by anybody who will observe the steps by which an ordinary "discount" is placed at the command of the borrower.

4. It has already been suggested that the use of deposits and checks is most highly developed among the English-speaking peoples. That the scattered branches of the English race should in this respect have followed the example of the mother country is not surprising; but the reasons for the difference in practice between England and the Continent are not so clear.† The difference itself, however, is strongly marked. The American or Englishman who is in the habit of receiving and mak-

---

* The weekly statement of the New York banks which is at hand as the above is revised, is a good illustration of the effect of such special conditions as are referred to above.

1885.	Loans.	Deposits.	Specie and Legal Tender.
October 10	331.9	387.3	137.
" 17	335.5	387.8	133.5
" 24	340.2	385.2	127.3
" 31	344.4	384.5	124.5

It appears from other evidence that during these three weeks $6.7 millions were withdrawn and paid into the United States Treasury and $3.6 millions sent to the interior. These withdrawals go far towards accounting for the reversed movement of deposits. See *Commercial and Financial Chronicle*.

† Mr. Bagehot plausibly conjectures that the immunity of England from foreign invasion and domestic revolution has made the growth of confidence possible, in a degree not permitted by the disturbed condition of the Continent for generations past. *Lombard Street*, p. 90. But this explanation appears unsatisfactory, in view of the frequently robust faith of continental traders and speculators, and of the ease with which English-speaking people establish deposit banks under the most untoward circumstances.

THE CHECK SYSTEM.

ing frequent payments avoids the keeping of cash in hand, deposits his receipts and pays all except the smallest sums by checks. As a consequence the establishment of a bank is an early symptom of the growth of trade in a small community of English blood. But even in large cities the French or German trader adheres to the old practice of keeping his own strong box; even large establishments adopt but slowly the habit of depositing. And in Italy, where banks of deposit flourished long before their introduction into England, they are sparingly used and make their way with some difficulty against a settled national habit. In these cases the silent choice of custom, which leads one people to prefer coin and another notes and a third to prefer a mixed currency, also leads to the personal custody and direct delivery of cash. The effect is to be seen, not only in the distribution of banking institutions, as to which the difference between the countries named is extreme, but also in the proportion which the deposits of the great banks in those countries respectively bear to their loans or private securities.* Upon the continent there is a marked preference for holding the engagement of the bank in the form of a note, rather than in that of a deposit, but in England or America, where the note is used for anything beyond the small purchases of everyday life, it is usually from necessity rather than choice.

---

* The published accounts of several great banks, at nearly the same time in October, 1885, afford the following comparative statement, the several currencies being reduced to dollars, at the rate of £1 or 25 francs for $5, and the amounts given in millions and tenths of millions :

	Loans.	*Deposits.*	*Notes.*
Bank of England,	111.4	148.3	128.5
" " France,	187.8	67.4	561.3
" " Belgium,	57.5	12.7	67.8
" " Netherlands,	34.2	5.9	79.9
Imp. Bank of Germany.	117.4	52.5	240.8
Nat. " " Italy,	83.1	22.5	109.3
Banks of New York,	331.9	387.3	9.9

36 CHAPTERS ON BANKING.

Peculiarities of national character are not the only conditions, however, which affect the use of deposits as currency in a given country. The extended use of a deposit and check system necessarily implies convenient access to banks and also a certain extended scale of operations. *Ceteris paribus*, then, the system will naturally be stronger where population is dense or communication easy, than in a sparsely settled country or where intercourse is difficult; manufactures, commerce, and general trade will afford it a better field than agriculture; and, comparing one period with another, its development in a country with increasing population and capital, and with diversified pursuits will be progressive and rapid. Accordingly we find that in the United States the city banks have extended the deposit system much farther than the country banks;* that in 1885 the system is developed much farther than in 1875; and that, to compare the banking of half a century ago with that of to-day, the United States Bank at the height of its prosperity was in this respect in as marked contrast with the national banks of to-day, as are the banks on the continent of Europe.† The full extent to which this development has now gone is seen, not in the mere amount to which bank deposits have risen on the average, but in the vast aggregate of transactions effected by this rapidly circulating medium, as

---

* The reports of the national banks for July 1, 1885, show the comparative standing of the city banks and of the country banks to have been as follows, taking equal amounts of capital, represented in each case by 100:

	City.	*Country.*
Capital	100	100
Loans	315	199
Individual deposits	319	157
Notes	36	59

† A comparison of the second United States Bank, at the height of its expansion in 1832, with the average condition of the city national banks

shown in the reports of the Clearing House. These reports contain the record of a mass of business, inconceivable in its amount and complexity, such as, it is certain, could not have come into existence without the aid of this powerful agent.

NOTE.

To illustrate the working of the Clearing House system, we will suppose the case of six banks carrying on business in the same town. On a given morning we will suppose the messengers of these banks to meet at the Clearing House, each bringing the checks received by his bank in deposit on the previous day, as follows:

No. 1, checks on No. 2,	$6,500		No. 4, checks on No. 1,	$8,750
" " " 3,	9,200		" " " 2,	4,700
" " " 4,	7,100		" " " 3,	6,740
" " " 5,	6,250		" " " 5,	5,820
" " " 6,	4,500		" " " 6,	5,140
	$33,550			$31,150
No. 2, checks on No. 1,	$7,800		No. 5, checks on No. 1,	$8,740
" " " 3,	4,100		" " " 2,	4,620
" " " 4,	5,760		" " " 3,	9,250
" " " 5,	6,340		" " " 4,	7,680
" " " 6,	5,870		" " " 6,	5,940
	$29,870			$36,230
No. 3, checks on No. 1,	$6,750		No. 6, checks on No. 1,	$3,700
" " " 2,	4,270		" " " 2,	4,100
" " " 4,	5,900		" " " 3,	6,740
" " " 5,	6,400		" " " 4,	9,250
" " " 6,	5,940		" " " 5,	7,850
	$29,260			$31,640

in July, 1885, taking the proportions for an equal amount of capital, shows the following contrast:

	1832.	*1885.*
Capital,	35 millions.	35 millions.
Loans,	70 "	110 "
Individual deposits,	9 "	112 "
Notes,	26 "	13 "

The sum of all the checks present is $191,700. If, now, we credit each bank with the checks which it presents against the others, and charge it with the checks presented by them against it, we shall find that No. 1 is charged with $35,740 and credited with $33,550, that No. 2 is charged with $24,190 and credited with $29,870, and so for the others, and, therefore, that,

No. 1 owes a balance of	$2,190	
No. 2 *is owed* " "		$5,680
No. 3 owes " "	6,770	
No. 4 " " "	4,540	
No. 5 *is owed* " "		3,570
No. 6 *is owed* " "		4,250
	$13,500	$13,500

If, then, the debtor banks, Nos. 1, 3, and 4, pay into the Clearing House the sums due from them amounting to $13,500 and the Clearing House pays out to the creditor banks, Nos. 2, 5, and 6, the sums due to them, of like amount, the result will be that every bank will, in effect, have collected payment of all the checks which it had received, and will have made payment of all the checks drawn against it. This settlement of checks amounting in all to $191,700 will have been made by the payment of $13,500, and transactions apparently involving thirty separate demands, each bank being the creditor of five others, will have been settled by a series of additions made at a central office followed by three payments to and three payments from a common fund.

An account of the transactions of the New York Clearing House, now by far the largest in existence, is given in the *Comptroller's Report for 1884*, p. 51. In 1884 that Clearing House settled the balances of sixty-one banks, and of the Assistant Treasurer of the United States. In 1881, the year of largest business, the average daily exchanges were $159,232,191, the transactions on some days approaching $300,000,000; and these exchanges were settled by the payment of balances averaging daily only $5,823,010. Since the foundation of the establishment in 1853, the balances actually paid have amounted on the average to only 4.4 per cent. of the exchanges effected. For the details of the process of clearing, see *Bolles, Practical Banking*, for the clearing houses of the United States; and *Gilbart, Principles and Practice of Banking*, for the London Clearing House.

CHAPTER IV.

BANKNOTES.

1. It has already been said that the notes of a bank are a liability distinguishable in form, but not in substance, from its deposits. The creditor of a bank of issue has his choice between taking the evidence of his right in the form of a note, and taking it in the form of a bank account. For his use the one form may be preferable to the other; if he desires to make payment in small sums, as for wages, he may prefer to take notes; if he is to make larger payments, or expects a little delay in the use of his funds, he is quite certain to prefer being credited with a deposit. But whatever his choice, the liability of the bank to make payment in money on demand is the same, and it is under the same necessity of providing itself with a reserve sufficient to meet any demand, which experience shows to be probable. To illustrate this part of the subject we will take again the account given on p. 26 and suppose the depositors to have drawn one-third of their deposits in notes of the bank, which have thus been thrown into circulation:

Liabilities.		*Resources.*	
Capital	$100,000	Loans	$269,000
Surplus	32,550	Bonds and stocks	20,000
Deposits	180,516	Real Estate	13,000
Notes	90,259	Other assets	13,000
		Reserve	88,325
	$403,325		$403,325

It is obvious from inspection that any demand upon the bank which weakens its reserve, whether the demand is from depositors or noteholders, produces the same effect; the security of the remaining liabilities, of whatever kind, is impaired and the same precautionary measures for replenishment will have to be taken. And so, if fresh loans are made, the relation of reserve to demand liabilities is altered, whether the loans are effected by an increase of deposits or of notes. The law does not always recognize this precise similarity of the two kinds of liability. It has sometimes required a reserve for the protection of notes alone, under the apparent impression that this must secure the solvency of the bank, and it sometimes makes a provision for a reserve of different amount for the notes, as in the national bank system of the United States, having in view the different degrees of strength of the probable demand for payment of notes and of deposits.* Apart, however, from considerations like the last, the two forms of liability seem to stand upon the same footing. The bank itself finds the same advantage in the one as in the other. Its profit is made from the securities which it holds, and whatever profit it makes beyond the mere interest on the investment of its capital, results from the holding of securities purchased by means of its credit; but the rate of this profit is in no way dependent upon the form in which that credit is transferred from one creditor to another.

The bank, in short, is interested simply in providing that form of credit which is most convenient for the use of the community on which it depends, for it is by that means that the greatest amount of securities can be held. Hence we see a remarkable difference in the issues of city and of country banks, carried on under the same system and with the same

---

* The national banks are now required by the Act of 1874, to have only a reserve of five per cent. for the protection of their notes, which is held by the Treasury as the central redeeming agency. *18 Statutes at Large, 123.* The bonds deposited to secure the circulation against insolvency, it is to be noticed, are in no sense a reserve and are not so described by the law.

privileges.* The deposit, transferred by check, is more convenient for large transactions than the note, being more expeditious and safer;† it is in the cities that transactions occur on the largest scale, as well as in the largest number; and it is in the cities, therefore, that the strongest need is felt of the medium of exchange best adapted for the transfer of great sums. It is in the cities, moreover, that the condition of convenient access to banks, needed for the full development of the deposit and check system, is realized in its highest degree. City banks, therefore, on the whole, use their right of circulating notes but sparingly as compared with country banks, and in some cases forego its use altogether, while their deposits attain an enormous expansion. Country banks, on the other hand, dealing on a smaller scale and in communities which have more need of a medium transferrible without recourse to the bank, find the expansion of their deposits much restricted in comparison with the circulation of their notes. It is for the same reason that, as time goes on, the relative importance of the banknote tends generally to diminish in comparison with

---

* See p. 36, *note*. A striking illustration of the same point is to be found in the condition of the national banks of New York city, compared with those of Massachusetts, outside of Boston, the amounts of capital being nearly the same. The figures here given only in millions, are for September 30, 1884. See *Comptroller's Report, 1884*.

	New York.	Massachusetts.
Capital	$46.2	$45.7
Loans and securities	239.	128.6
Notes	13.2	35.8
Individual deposits	184.6	45.4

† The safety of the deposit is due to the fact that the check, being usually payable "to order," especially when the amount is considerable, cannot be drawn or credited to its holder unless endorsed by the payee. If lost or stolen, therefore, it cannot be paid unless the bank is deceived by a forged endorsement, in which case the loss falls upon the bank itself. Banknotes, however, being payable to bearer, are nearly as difficult to trace as money.

that of deposits. The swift development of modern commerce is expanding in high proportion the field for the most convenient and efficient medium, while the small transactions, in which notes find their use, are growing in slower ratio. It becomes more and more the business of banks, therefore, to extend the use of their credit in the form of deposits, the increase in their issue of notes being, in the most progressive communities, no longer a matter of great concern.*

2. That governments have so frequently felt it their duty to take measures for the protection of the holders of banknotes against the insolvency of the bank, but have so seldom legislated for the protection of depositors, is probably due to several reasons. Legislators have generally failed to perceive the similarity of the two kinds of liability; moreover, the appropriate measures for the protection of the noteholders are more obvious and of easier application; and it is doubtless true also that depositors, as a class, are better informed and can more easily protect themselves, and so have less claim upon the sympathy and guardianship of the legislature. At all events, provision for the safety of notes is not infrequently made by law, and when made is apt to consist either of the easily understood requirement of a certain reserve of cash for the payment of the notes, or of a preferential claim to some portion of the assets, allowed to the holders of notes in case a bank becomes insolvent.

The effect of provisions for giving holders of notes a preferred claim may be illustrated easily, if we take the statement of account last given, and, without any change of liabilities, suppose the bank to have been led to make a change of investments and to diminish its other assets and its reserve, until the account stands as follows:

---

* Compare the condition of the State banks from 1834 to 1863 with that of the national banks in recent years. *Comptroller's Report for 1876*, p. 94. See especially the remarkable development of the New York banks during the former period. *Ibid*, p. 102.

Liabilities.		Resources.	
Capital	$100,000	Loans	$217,000
Surplus	32,550	Bond and stocks	101,000
Deposits	180,516	Real estate	13,000
Notes	90,259	Other assets	4,000
		Reserve	68,325
	$403,325		$403,325

The liabilities of the bank are plainly of two classes; the liability to stockholders for capital and surplus, and the liability to outside creditors for deposits and notes. If the affairs of the bank were to be wound up, by reason of losses or for any other reason, it is clear that in case of any deficiency of resources, the outside creditors should be paid in full first, and that only the residue after such payment can be said to be the property of the stockholders and so divisible among them. If, for example, it proved that by reason of failures and losses, the loans, bonds, real estate and other assets, instead of being worth $335,000, which was their cost, were worth only $225,000; we should then have a total of resources amounting to $293,325, leaving, after the payment of deposits and notes, only $22,550 to be divided among the stockholders, the disaster having swept away their supposed surplus, and about three-quarters of their capital. We may go further and suppose the depreciation to have reduced the value of the total resources to $250,000, in which case the creditors must be satisfied with a dividend of a fraction more than 92 per cent.* and the stockholders are seen to have lost all that they had embarked in the business.

---

* If we suppose the law to make the stockholders liable as individuals for the debts of the bank, they would under these circumstances be subject to an assessment, in order to make full payment to the depositors and noteholders. For the liability of stockholders under the national bank system of the United States, see *Revised Statutes*, § 5151. See also *Comptroller's Report*, 1884, 44.

In these cases the depositors, holders of notes and other outside creditors, all, in short, who can properly be regarded as creditors in the settlement, stand upon the same footing, one with another, and have similar rights, neither class having any preference unless some special legislative provision intervenes to that end. We may now suppose that the legislature, for the protection of the holders of notes, had given them a right to be paid in full in preference to other creditors, if the assets of a bank in liquidation should fall short.* In that case, from the total resources amounting to $250,000, we should first have the notes paid in full, amounting to $90,259; and then the remaining $159,741 would be divided among the depositors, giving them a dividend of a little more than 88 per cent.

A provision of law, then, giving the holders of notes a preferred claim to the assets of the bank would be a natural and easy method of insuring this class of creditors, except in case of a very large issue or a very bad failure. But we may suppose the legislature to wish to go farther than this and to give the noteholders, not a general claim in preference to others, but a claim to specific property of the bank, supposed to be of solid value and sufficient to insure payment of the notes in any case. Thus, to return to the account on page 43, it appears that the bank holds bonds and stocks to the amount of $101,000 as a part of its securities. Suppose, then, that the law requires the bank to hold these bonds and stocks pledged to secure the ultimate payment of its $90,259 of notes. Under such an arrangement, the securities would not cease to be the property of the bank and the earnings of the securities would remain, as before, a part of the profits of the bank. The pledged property would be enjoyed, however, subject to the provision that in case of the failure of the bank, the proceeds of the securities should be applied first to the payment of the

---

* *E. g.* see New Hampshire *Compiled Statutes* of 1853, ch. 148 § 30.

outstanding notes. If the law should go farther and provide that only certain approved classes of securities should be used for this purpose, and that the securities pledged should be lodged for safe-keeping in the hands of some public officer, the substance of the transaction would still be unchanged. It would still remain a simple case of the specific appropriation of a certain part of the property of the bank to the payment of a particular class of its liabilities in a given contingency. The essential structure of the bank would be unchanged and the sources of its profits would be neither more nor fewer than they were in the absence of this pledge of securities.

The method just described, of protecting the issue of notes by a deposit of securities in the hands of some public officer, is that which was adopted by the state of New York in 1838, and was long known as the "free banking" system. Many other States followed the example of New York, and finally in 1863 the New York plan was adopted by Congress as the basis for the national banking system.*

If, now, we vary our suppositions so far as to imagine the property pledged for the protection of the notes to consist, not wholly of securities, but of securities to a certain amount and of specie for all notes issued in excess thereof, we shall have in substance the provision made by law in 1844 for the protection of the notes of the Bank of England.

3. Beside other reasons already adverted to, for seeking legislative protection for banknotes, the belief has been common that banks are under a special and dangerous temptation to overissue notes, thus causing their depreciation with loss to the public. The question whether really convertible notes *can* be issued in excess has been the subject of much wearisome

---

* For an account of the New York system and its adoption by other states, see *Comptroller's Report* for 1876, 23-36.

and futile discussion,* tending to secure for the notes far more than their proper share of attention. It has already been shown, however, that the question whether notes shall be issued or not, is one which in modern banking is not settled affirmatively by the bank, but by the creditor, who determines for himself and with an eye to his own convenience, whether to hold his right, as against the bank, in the form of a note or of a deposit. If he and creditors generally prefer the latter, the bank cannot force its notes into circulation. The really serious question would be whether the bank can extend the use of its credit, by deposits as well as by notes, in excess. This is as much as to ask whether the bank can go too far in the purchase of securities, or in other words, unduly stimulate borrowers, the making of loans being the purpose for which the bank extends its credit. But this question cannot be answered without qualification. If we observe any period of ten years, we shall find some years in which banks have found the public depressed and spiritless, to such a degree that, with every motive for increasing their business, it has been found impossible to find sound commercial paper in sufficient amount. So far from being able to extend their credit in excess, banks have at such times often reduced their capital because employment for it could not be found. Other years we shall find in which the public spirit was buoyant and adventurous, and in which the banks have fostered and increased the general tendency to speculation, by the facility with which they have given the use of their credit. It is true then that banks cannot extend their liabilities of either sort except in response to a demand from the public; it is also true that in certain states of business this demand may be unduly stimulated by their action, and that issues made in response to such a factitious

---

* For convenient citations on this subject, see Walker on *Money*, ch. xix.

BANKNOTES. 47

demand may be said to be in excess of the proper needs of the community. In any such expansion of bank credit, however, banknotes play the least important part.*

NOTE.

Of the writers on banking, McLeod, *Theory and Practice of Banking*, has made the most careful analysis of the exchange which underlies every banking operation. Notwithstanding eccentricities of method and style, his exposition of the real meaning of "loans" and the ambiguities incident to our use of that term, the origin and purport of bank liabilities and the substantial identity of the liabilities for deposits and notes, is clear and important, and might be cited in confirmation at many points in these pages. Reference may also be made with advantage to McLeod's smaller work, *Elements of Banking*.

Among earlier discussions attention is specially called to a striking letter by James Pennington, *Tooke's History of Prices*, II. 369, in which the strong analogy between the deposit accounts of the London private bankers and the notes of the country bankers is forcibly stated and explained.

---

* The condition of the national banks in December, 1878, was one of great depression and may be compared with their expanded state in October, 1881.

	December 6, 1878.	*October 1, 1881.*
Capital	$464.9	$463.8
Loans	826.	1173.8
Deposits	598.8	1071.
Notes	303.3	320.2

CHAPTER V.

THE NATIONAL BANKS OF THE UNITED STATES.

1. THE national banking system of the United States owes its existence to the civil war. Although in the majority of the States the banks incorporated under State authority were badly organized and insecure, and although even such as were on a solid foundation could enjoy only a restricted local credit, the current of opinion before the war was by no means favorable to any consolidation of banking interests. Discontent with existing systems more frequently took the form of opposition to the existence of any banks of issue at all; the party then apparently holding permanent control of the administration cherished with pride the traditions of its victorious struggle with the United States bank, and of its devotion to a gold currency; and probably neither the friends nor the opponents of banking would have thought at that time of finding in the government of the United States a power able to reorganize upon a common plan the note issues of all the States.

The imperious necessity of finding a market for United States bonds for the supply of a Treasury drained by war was the favoring condition needed for such a reorganization, and the assumption of unusual powers by the United States government, which had become habitual under the pressure of a struggle for existence, made the resort to federal authority practicable. In 1860 a majority of the people would have thought the establishment of a third United States bank dangerous and of doubtful constitutionality. In 1863 a system of national banks, indefinitely more powerful than the bank which

NATIONAL BANKS OF THE UNITED STATES. 49

waged an almost equal war with Jackson, was established with widespread, although not unanimous, consent, and without solid opposition except that of some existing interests threatened or alarmed by the change. It was, indeed, urged by some that, as the wants of the Treasury were the real controlling motive in the establishment of the new system, it would be better for the government to issue its own notes to the extent of the proposed bank circulation, and to occupy the whole of the field, of which it had already taken a part, and so enjoy the full advantage of a non-interest-bearing debt. Fortunately these views gained little support, and the dangerous expedient of relying solely upon the issue of government notes was not pushed beyond the limit of possible return to specie payment.*

2. The adoption of a system of national banks, having their notes secured by the deposit of United States bonds, had been proposed by the Secretary of the Treasury in 1861, and strongly urged by him in 1862. An act for the purpose was passed in February, 1863,† but in many points of detail this proved to be so unsatisfactory and incomplete, that only 134 banks were organized under it in the next nine months and the number had risen to less than 450 in sixteen months. A revised act, making important changes, was therefore passed in June, 1864,‡ and ample provision having been made, under which banks chartered by the States could be reorganized as national banks, the extension of the new system went on rapidly. Its adoption was further stimulated by an act laying a tax of ten per cent. on all notes of State banks paid out by any bank after July 1, 1866; ‖ and at that date the number

---

* See *Report on the National Bank Currency Act*, written by the late John E. Williams, and made to the New York Clearing House banks, November 28, 1863.
† 12 *Statutes at Large*, 665.
‡ 13 *Statutes at Large*, 99.
‖ 13 *Statutes at Large*, 469.

of national banks, then 1634, easily reached the level at which it stood for several years.*

The general provisions of the national bank system† restrict the right of issuing notes to the national banks, but do not interfere with the performance of any of the other functions of banking by banks chartered by State authority, or by private banks. The issue of notes is to be secured by a deposit of registered bonds of the United States, the bonds being transferred to and held by the Treasurer at Washington, but the interest thereon collected by the banks, whose property the bonds continue to be. The deposit of bonds under these provisions entitles the bank making such deposit to receive from the Comptroller of the Currency, who has the general charge of the system, notes to the amount of ninety per cent. of the market value of the bonds deposited, but not exceeding ninety per cent. of their par value. These notes when received are in blank, certifying only the fact that the security for them is in the hands of the government; but when signed by the proper officers of the bank, they become its promises to pay upon demand, and can then be issued for circulation. They are, of course, to be paid by the issuing bank whenever presented, are also to be received in payment by all other national banks, and can be paid to or be used in payments by the government in all cases where specie is not required by law; but they have never been a legal tender as between individuals.

---

* A summary statement of the number and condition of the national banks, at four or five dates in every year, and for every year since the adoption of the system, is given annually in the *Comptroller's Report.*

† The legislation on this subject down to 1873 is embodied in §§ 5133-5243 of the *Revised Statutes* of 1878. The subsequent acts of importance are the Compromise Act of 1874, 18 *Statutes at Large*, 123; the Resumption Act of 1875, *Ibid*, 296; the act of 1880 concerning gold banks, 21 *Id.* 66; and the act of 1882 extending the existence of the banks, 22 *Id.* 162.

These provisions have secured for the notes a uniform value and give to the notes of every bank an unimpeded circulation in every part of the Union. If, indeed, the law, as in the act of 1863, still made no further provision for redemption than to require every bank to redeem its own notes when presented at its own counter, the return of notes for payment and their substantial convertibility would be nearly destroyed. But the law of 1864 made provision for redemption by all banks at agencies in the principal cities, and this arrangement continued in force until June, 1874,* when the present system was adopted, making the Treasury of the United States the sole redeeming agency for all of the national banks, and requiring every bank to keep in the Treasury, to be used in redemption of its notes, a reserve equal to five per cent. of its circulation. The chief effect of the present system of redemption, however, is the easy removal from circulation of notes which are worn, soiled, or otherwise unfit for use.† For the establishment of a system which should test effectively and continuously the power of every bank to convert its notes into specie on demand, it would probably be necessary to require that no national bank should pay out any notes except its own.‡ For the general purpose of maintaining the convertibility of the aggregate note issue of the banks and its ready diminution

---

* 18 *Statutes at Large*, 123.

† During the year ending with October, 1884, the notes received at the redemption agency amounted to $136,577,732; of them $33,080,300, an unusual proportion, were returned to the banks as "fit for circulation." *Comptroller's Report* for 1884, p. 71.

‡ Such a prohibition was the basis on which the "Suffolk bank system" of New England rested, from 1819 to 1866, and maintained at par a note circulation which had otherwise but slender provision for convertibility. Massachusetts *General Statutes* of 1860, ch. 57, § 55; but compare also § 124. And see D. R. Whitney, *The Suffolk Bank*.

when required by the condition of business, the present arrangement is well devised.

The national banknote when issued is the promise of the issuing bank, and must be punctually met by it, as any other liability must be. The note, however, carries with it certain engagements binding upon the government of the United States. The provision for redemption at the Treasury binds the government to pay on demand all notes when presented in due form, and not merely notes to the extent of the reserve. And in case of the failure of a bank, the law provides for the immediate redemption of all its notes at the Treasury. The government has thus made itself fully liable in any event for the whole amount of the notes. On the other hand, it has taken ample security for its reimbursement, by requiring the deposit of bonds as above stated, by requiring that this deposit shall be increased if the value of the bonds declines, by the provision for a reserve of cash to be held by the Treasury, and also by taking for itself a first lien upon all the assets of a bank for the purpose of making good any possible deficiency in the security already provided. An ingenious provision in the act of 1882 also secures for the government any gain that may ultimately accrue from the destruction of notes while outstanding, or the failure for any reason to call for their redemption. And finally, although the expenses of printing the notes (but not of engraving the plates) of superintending the system, and of providing for the safe-keeping of the bonds deposited, are paid by the government, these charges are offset by a tax of one per cent. per annum on the average amount of notes in circulation. On the whole, therefore, whatever may be gained by the banks from this system, it cannot be said that the liability of the government is onerous.

3. Although in its general theory the national banking system is one of "free banking," under which the business of banking in all its branches shall be open to all persons who comply with the formalities provided by the law, it was never-

theless felt to be dangerous to allow the issue of an unlimited circulation so long as the currency remained irredeemable. The attempt to restrict what was in theory free led, therefore, to a series of contradictory and in some respects remarkable provisions.

Without restricting the establishment of banks, the acts of 1863 and 1864 limited the aggregate amount of notes to $300,000,000; and while no bank was allowed to issue notes exceeding in amount its capital stock, every bank was required to deposit bonds amounting to at least one-third of its capital. Apprehending that the rapid reorganization of the numerous State banks in the Eastern and Middle States might fill up the prescribed aggregate of circulation, before the West should be able to organize a due proportion of banking capital, the act of 1863 also required one-half of the total circulation to be apportioned among the States according to their representative population, and one-half "having due regard to the existing bank-capital and resources." The reluctance of the banks to reorganize as national banks, however, caused the omission of this provision in the act of 1864; but Congress in 1865, while encouraging the immediate reorganization of existing banks, revived the provisions for apportioning the aggregate circulation and fixed a narrower limit for that of banks of the larger class.

As early as November, 1868, notes had been issued to nearly the amount allowed by law, and the West and South soon began to complain of the difficulty of organizing banks, without the right of issue, in sparsely settled States. In 1870 a chance was offered for the increase of banknotes without increase of the aggregate paper currency of the country, by the contemplated payment of certain obligations of the Treasury hitherto used by the banks as a part of their reserves, for which legal tender notes would now have to be substituted and thus withdrawn from circulation. Congress therefore seized the opportunity of extending the aggregate limit of notes for circulation by $54,000,000, to be apportioned among States having less than their due proportion, and further required that, after this increase of note circulation should have been made, a redistribution of the right of issue should be made by the withdrawal to the extent of $25,000,000, from States having more than their due proportion, and the apportionment of the same among States having less. The limit for each bank thereafter organized was reduced to half a million dollars, and provision was even made for allowing the removal of existing banks to States having less than their due proportion of note circulation.

By the end of 1873 the new limit of $354,000,000 was nearly filled and finding itself impelled to legislate upon the currency by the financial revulsion of that year, Congress after painful debate elaborated the Compromise Act of June, 1874, in which provision was made for the immediate withdrawal of circulation from States having an excess and its distribution among banks in States having a deficiency, as fast as application should be made by the latter, to the extent of $55,000,000, including the $25,000,000 already provided for. Arrangements for carrying this act into execution, however, had hardly been made, when this series of crude and futile measures was brought to an abrupt close, by the hasty passage of the act of January, 1875, for the resumption of specie payments. This act fortunately swept away all the provisions limiting and apportioning the aggregate amount of banknotes to be authorized, as well as those calling for the withdrawal and redistribution of issues already authorized, and thus established the national banks for the first time on the basis of freedom, required by the theory of the original measure. No change was needed to adapt the system to a resumption of specie payments, its details having been arranged at the outset so as to admit of easy translation into terms of specie.

4. In its regulation of the discount and deposit business of the national banks, the law does not follow the example of

some previous legislation, by fixing a limit to the amount of securities to be held by any bank,* but simply prescribes a minimum reserve to be held for the protection of the liability for deposits. For banks in sixteen "reserve cities," named in the act of Congress,† the reserve must be twenty-five per cent. of the deposits; for all other banks, fifteen per cent. The provisions for determining what shall be counted as reserve are, however, less simple. The general requirement is that it shall be "lawful money," or in other words specie or legal tender notes of the United States, so long as a paper legal tender exists. But Clearing House certificates, which represent lawful money specially deposited for the purposes of the Clearing House association, of which the bank owning them may be a member, and the cash reserve of five per cent. of its circulation, which every bank is required to keep in the Treasury, are also to be counted as a part of the reserve against deposits. And it is further provided that, for any bank in a redemption city one-half of its reserve may consist of cash deposits in the city of New York, and for any bank outside of the redemption cities three-fifths of its reserve may in like manner consist of deposits with banks in those cities.

The permission thus given, to count certain demands for cash as cash itself, has a marked effect upon the composition of the reserve held by the banks as an aggregate, and therefore upon the strength of the whole mass of banks at any given moment. If we take the returns of the national banks for October 1, 1883, we find their deposits amounting in the aggregate to

---

* See *e. g.* Massachusetts *General Statutes* of 1860, c. 57, § 25; New York *Revised Statutes* of 1859, II. 518; Maine *Revised Statutes* of 1857 ch. 47, § 19.

† The reserve cities are Boston, Albany, New York, Philadelphia, Pittsburgh, Baltimore, Washington, New Orleans, Louisville, Cincinnati, Cleveland, Detroit, Chicago, Milwaukee, St. Louis, and San Francisco. The list included Leavenworth, until the passage of the act of March 1, 1872.

1168.7 millions of dollars, requiring a reserve of 234.4 millions. They are returned as holding 328.9 millions of reserve in all, and were therefore, on the average, far above the legal minimum. But this great apparent reserve was composed as follows:

Specie	107.8 millions.
Other lawful money	80.6 "
Redemption fund	15.6 "
Due from reserve cities	124.9 "
Total	$328.9 "

Of actual cash, then, the banks of the country at this date held but 204 millions, much less than the amount of reserve required for their liabilities,—the remaining sum, which apparently made their condition remarkably strong, consisting merely of debts due from one bank to another. The ability of the mass of banks, therefore, to meet the pressure of a financial crisis was dependent on the ability of the debtor banks to pay upon demand the sums deposited with them and relied upon by the others as a part of their reserve, or in other words on the ability of the banks of New York city to meet their liabilities.* The reserve of those banks, however, on which all the

---

* The reserve October 1, 1881, was divided between city and country, and classified as follows:

Classification of Reserve.

	Reserve required.	Reserve held.	Specie.	Legal Tender etc.	5 p'r c't fund.	Due from banks.
New York City,	67.2 m.	62.5 m.	50.6 m.	10.9 m.	1.0 m.	....
Other Res. cities,	83.9	100.8	34.6	21.9	3.7	40.6
Country	76.1	158.4	27.5	27.1	11.4	92.4
Totals,	227.2	321.7	112.7	59.9	16.1	133.0

The published reports make it probable, although not certain, that in the middle of October, 1873, when the reserves of the New York banks had fallen to less than eleven per cent. of their liabilities and payments had been generally suspended, the reserves of the rest of the country were above the line required by law.

others rested, was but little above the legal minimum at the date named, and sometimes under similar conditions has been below that point, so that with an apparently high reserve for the country at large, there was such weakness at the central and most exposed point as to seriously impair the value of this precaution.

The relation of the New York banks to the other banks of the country, as the depository of their reserves, is plainly quite analogous to that of the Bank of England as the depository of the joint stock and private banks of London, and the effects seen in the weakening of reserves and the concentration of risks is the same in both cases.* As regards the national banks the tendency to centralize the reserves, favored by the law, is heightened by the practice, long established among the New York banks and also existing elsewhere, of inviting deposits by country banks by the payment of interest.† The opportunity of converting a barren reserve into an interest-bearing resource, and yet counting it as reserve, has always been attractive and has caused an habitual transfer from the country banks to those of New York, sometimes estimated at not far from $80,000,000. The employment given to the funds thus held subject to call is a topic of serious interest on which it is impossible to enter now.

5. For the enforcement of the provision as to reserve, the law provides that whenever the reserve of any bank falls below the prescribed limit, the bank shall neither "increase its liabilities by making any new loans or discounts," otherwise than by the purchase of sight bills of exchange, nor shall it make

---

* See Bagehot's *Lombard Street*, 160-173; Dun's *British Banking Statistics*, 129.

† This practice was condemned by resolution by the banks of the New York Clearing House in 1857, 1873, and 1884. See *Banker's Magazine*, April, 1858, p. 322; *Commercial and Financial Chronicle*, November, 1873, p. 651; *Banker's Magazine*, August, 1884, p. 129. Resolutions alone, however, have never proved to be a cure.

any dividend, until the reserve has been restored to its due proportion. The Comptroller of the Currency is also authorized to notify any bank whose reserve is insufficient that it must be made good, and in case of failure to comply within thirty days, he may, with the concurrence of the Secretary of the Treasury, appoint a receiver to wind up the business of the bank. Although the ample discretion thus given to the Comptroller has been used with great moderation,* the prohibition of further discounts, when the reserve falls below a given point, makes a hard and fast line, the approach to which never fails to cause uneasiness and in some conditions of affairs is viewed with serious alarm. In any actual crisis, the declaration that in a given contingency like this the usual accommodation of the public must stop and liquidation must begin, is the surest means of increasing the pressure for loans and of thus converting a crisis into a panic. For ease in operation and greater safety, some more elastic provision is needed, which shall insure a sufficiently high average of reserve and yet make no harsh break in operations at a given point. The Bank of England has in its hands a superior instrument for this purpose in the sliding scale of discount, by which it can encourage or discourage borrowers and thus deplete or replenish its reserve, without ceasing its operations altogether at any point yet reached. This expedient, however, is inapplicable in the United States, partly because of the traditional prejudice against the adjustment of rates of discount by the demand in the market, widely prevalent among our people, and partly because Congress has been obliged by probable lack of authority to forego the establishment of a general law respecting interest, and to recognize in each State the rates there prescribed by the local legislature. A suggestion of an elastic limit is contained in certain provisions of the German bank law which,

---

* See the course pursued in September and October, 1873, when the reserve of the banks of New York were far below the line and both city and country banks had suspended payment.

after a prescribed line, tax the operations without, however, prohibiting them; but this expedient, devised long after the establishment of the national banking system by Congress, has not yet had such trial as to thoroughly test its capabilities.

6. Much controversy has been excited by the question as to the rate of profits which the national banks have obtained from their right of issuing notes secured by a deposit of bonds. It has already been shown that their case is in no respect different as regards profits from that of banks which use their credit in the form of deposits, in order to make investments in interest-bearing securities. The notion often entertained, that the national banks have some peculiar opportunity of making a double profit, "by receiving both interest earned by "their bonds, and interest earned by the loan of the notes "issued upon the bonds," overlooks the fact that every bank uses, as its means for obtaining securities, its capital and whatever credit it can employ in addition.* The conclusive practical answer to the idea of a supposed double profit is to be found, however, in the conduct of the banks themselves, especially since the passage of the act of 1874, already referred to. That act, recognizing the desire of many banks to reduce their circulation and secure possession of their bonds, provided that any bank might deposit "lawful money" with the Treasurer of the United States to enable him to redeem its notes, and thereupon withdraw *pro tanto* the bonds deposited, provided the amount of its bonds left in deposit were not reduced below $50,000.† Several important national banks had never chosen

---

* The actual profit earned by the banks from their right of circulation was estimated by the Comptroller of the Currency in 1883 not to exceed $46 on $90,000 of notes. See *Comptroller's Report*, 1883, 13.

† For an objection made at the Treasury to the working of this provision, see *Finance Report*, 1880, 331; 1881, 221. For the connection between this provision and the "bank panic" of March, 1881, see *Comptroller's Report* for 1881, p. 39; *Atlantic Monthly*, February, 1882, p. 195.

to issue notes, although required by the law to maintain a deposit of bonds; under this provision a considerable number reduced their notes to the $45,000 which the required minimum deposit of bonds would support. The withdrawals of notes continued for several years, and although new banks were formed and the note circulation increased in some sections, under the authority for free banking given by the resumption act, the total banking capital and note circulation alike declined, until the summer of 1878. Both increased after the resumption of specie payments, but the circulation of bank notes, although open to all banks, and to any amount, never reached its old point. This course of things was entirely inconsistent with the existence of large profits arising from the issue of notes under the national system. It is impossible to believe that, if such profits were reaped, existing banks would have neglected or renounced the opportunity of making them, or that the multitude of private bankers, and of State banks would have failed to seize upon an opportunity which was free to all,* by organizing under the national system.

That a good rate of profit has been made by the national banks upon their general business is no doubt true. Especially during the period of irredeemable paper their harvest was large, as is usually the case with the dealers in money and credit during a period of non-payment and of fluctuation. The law has from the first required of every bank that a part of its profits should be reserved, until an surplus amounting to one-fifth of the capital should be accumulated. A solid foundation was laid for their surplus in many cases, by the sale at a high premium of the gold held by State banks before their reorganization, and retained by them until the adoption of the paper system had plainly become definitive. The banks

---

* Until the spring of 1881, two-thirds of the bonds held by the banks to secure their circulation bore interest at not less five per cent. and a considerable amount at six.

had thus on the average accumulated the surplus required by law before the end of 1869, since which time their accumulation has increased or diminished as the times were prosperous, or the reverse, their surplus varying from 26.6 per cent. of the capital in October, 1875, to 25 per cent. in December, 1878, and again to 28.3 per cent. in December, 1883.* The annual dividends paid from earnings after the reservation for surplus, also stood at their highest point during the period of most rapid accumulation, and have varied from a maximum of 10.58 per cent. of the capital to a minimum of 7.59 per cent. Without doubt this rate of dividends shows a prosperous business, but how far the prosperity is due to privileges enjoyed under the national system may be judged, from the near approach which State banks make to national banks in their earning capacity.†

7. There is no doubt that, in adopting the national banking system the majority of Congress understood themselves to be establishing the agency by which the sole paper currency of the country should be issued in the future. The legal tender issues were still regarded as a temporary expedient, resting upon

---

* For many years the largest surplus held has belonged to a bank which issues no notes, but has accumulated many times the amount of its capital. It is true in general that the banks of largest surplus have not owed it to their issue of notes.

† In New York, where there are nearly 100 banks organized under the laws of the State, the percentage of surplus and undivided profits to capital under the two systems respectively was in September, 1879, 1882, and 1884 as follows:

	National banks.	State banks.
September, 1879	.45	.37
" 1882	.58	.52
" 1884	.57	.54

See *Report of State Banking Department* for 1884, and *Comptroller's Report*.

the overwhelming exigency of the moment for their justification; the bank act is entitled "An act to provide a national currency," emphasizing by its title the permanence of the substitute which was to fill the place left vacant by the legal tender notes when paid; and the text of the act plainly looks forward to the return of specie payment, which should leave specie the only tender for debt.* Establishing a permanent system of banks Congress undertook to surround them by the ordinary safeguards needful to give them full credit, providing minutely for their organization and superintendence, and for the publication of their accounts at rather short intervals, and laying down rules, wholesome so far as they go, restricting the kinds of business in which the banks should engage. It was provided also that the shareholders should be responsible ratably for the debts of the banks, each to the amount of his stock in addition to the capital actually invested by him.†

A system of banks thus guarded and under the charge of

---

*In 1870 when the return to specie payments finally seemed to have been postponed indefinitely, an act was passed authorizing the establishment of gold banks, issuing notes redeemable in gold coin, and secured by the deposit of "United States bonds bearing interest payable in gold" with the treasurer of the United States. The notes were not to exceed eighty per cent. of the value of the bonds, and were not to be subject to those provisions of law which then limited the aggregate circulation of bank notes. Several gold banks were organized, chiefly in the Pacific States; but after the return to specie payments the distinction between them and other banks ceasing to be of importance, provision was made by the act of 1880 for their conversion into national banks of the usual type. 21 *Statutes at Large*, 66.

† From this liability to contribution beyond the amount invested, the law made an exception in favor of the stockholders of any existing State bank, having a capital of not less than five millions and a surplus of twenty per cent., in case of its reorganization as a national bank. This exception was made in order to secure the adhesion of the Bank of Commerce of New York city,— the only bank in the United States which could meet these conditions.

the government itself could hardly be treated by Congress as unworthy of being entrusted with the public funds, as the State banks had been under the independent treasury act of 1846, and provision was therefore made for designating banks as depositories of public money when occasion should require, and for their employment as financial agents of the government, upon their giving satisfactory security, by the deposit of United States bonds and otherwise, for the faithful discharge of these functions. The framers of the measure no doubt looked forward at one time to a more consolidated system of banks, and to a closer intimacy with the government than was in fact established; but their action as it stands marks an extraordinary change of policy, made under the pressure of war, by a government which, hardly more than two years before, trusted no agency whatever with the custody of its funds, recognized no medium of payment except specie, and carefully disclaimed all connection with, or responsibility for, any possible system of banks.

CHAPTER VI.

THE BANK OF ENGLAND.

1. The Bank of England owes its origin to the financial straits to which the government of William and Mary found itself reduced in carrying on its war with Louis the Fourteenth. The revenues of the kingdom were small, the public credit weak, and the very title of the dynasty unsettled. The growing wealth and business of the country had caused private banking houses to spring up. The paper given by these houses to their creditors had acquired a circulation, limited indeed, but sufficient to show its convenience, and projects for the establishment of a public institution on the scale, if not on the model, of the great continental banks, had been discussed for many years.* Under these circumstances, as an expedient for raising a million sterling, for which no other resource could be found, the government in 1694 adopted the scheme proposed by William Patterson, a Scotch adventurer, and proposed to Parliament that a loan should be offered for public subscription and made attractive by a grant of incorporation with banking privileges, to be enjoyed by the subscribers and their successors. The measure seems to have been contested chiefly, although not wholly, on party grounds, and was passed after a

---

* McLeod, *Theory and Practice of Banking*, I, 210, prints a "goldsmith's note" which is still preserved, dated 1684. And see *Macaulay's History*, VII, 134. The plan of establishing a national bank had been agitated as far back as 1660.

severe struggle, and thus the Bank of England came into existence as a Whig corporation.*

The act of 1694 provided for a loan to the government of £1,200,000, bearing interest at eight per cent., and incorporated the subscribers, with this amount of nominal capital, as the Governor and Company of the Bank of England,—a title which has never been changed. The corporation was empowered to deal in coin, bullion and exchange, and to lend upon security, but was forbidden to deal in merchandise in any form. It could not borrow nor give security by bill, bond or agreement, for an amount exceeding its capital; no provision was made for the transfer of its bills, "obligatory or of credit" except by indorsement; nor was any monopoly created in its favor. In this form the charter of the Bank gave little promise of its future importance. Three years later, however, the necessities of the government and the embarrassments of the Bank, which had been obliged to suspend payment in 1696, led to a revision of the charter, in which the outlines of the great structure appear.† The issue of notes payable to bearer on demand was authorized, thus laying the foundation for a true banknote circulation,‡ the monopoly of corporate organization was granted by providing that, during the continuance of the

---

* The fiscal character of the measure is very well shown by its title. "An Act for granting to their Majesties several duties upon tonnage of Ships and Vessels, and upon Beer, Ale and other Liquors, for securing certain Recompenses and Advantages in the said Act mentioned, to such Persons as shall voluntarily advance the sum of fifteen hundred thousand Pounds towards carrying on the War against *France.* 5 *William and Mary, ch. 20.*

For the political relations of the Bank of England, at and after its establishment, see *Macaulay's History,* VII, 147.

† 8 *and* 9 *William* III. ch. 20.

‡ The notes issued under the act of 1794 appear to have borne interest, and being made to order, could have had but a limited circulation No notes of less than £20 were issued until the act of 1759 authorized the issue of notes for £15 and £10.

charter, no other bank or corporation in the nature of a bank, should be allowed in the kingdom; and on the other hand the capital was doubled by a fresh advance from the stockholders to the government, and the interest payable by the latter was reduced to six per cent.

From this point the growth of the Bank and the increase of its influence were rapid. The corporation became the chief depository of the government moneys, and the agent of the Treasury in many financial operations. In 1720 it carried on a mad struggle with the South Sea Company for the control of the business of refunding the national debt, and managed, although with difficulty, to save its own credit in the crisis which destroyed its rival. Further loans to the government and additions to the capital of the Bank were made in quick succession. In 1722 its capital stood at nearly nine millions, and it was also able to establish from its profits the surplus fund now called "the Rest," and thus to save its dividends from great fluctuation. In 1782 the capital had risen to more than eleven millions and a half, and in 1816 it had risen to £14,553,000, at which figure it has stood ever since. Of the loan to the government, which had risen in nearly the same proportion as the capital, one-fourth was repaid in 1834, reducing it to £11,015,100, which is its present amount. By the year 1750 the government had succeeded in reducing the interest on most of its debt to the Bank to three per cent., and it has since used the opportunity afforded by the periodical necessity for a renewal of the charter, to lessen still more the burden of its interest, by requiring from the Bank an annual bonus and other pecuniary concessions, in consideration of the extension of its monopoly.

2. This monopoly, dating, as has just been said, from the act of 1697, and confirmed by the act of 1709, was further defined by the act of 1742* as the right of "exclusive banking,"

---

* 16 *Anne, ch* 22; 15 *George* II, ch. 13.

the true intent being, as is declared in the latter year, that "no other Bank shall be erected, established or allowed by "Parliament, and that it shall not be lawful for any Body "Politick or Corporate whatsoever, erected or to be erected, "or for any other Persons whatsoever, united or to be united, "in Covenants or Partnership, exceeding the number of six "Persons, in that Part of *Great Britain* called *England*, to "borrow, owe, or take up, any Sum or Sums of Money on their "Bills or Notes, payable at Demand, or at any less Time than "six Months from the borrowing thereof, during the Continu-"ance of such said Privilege to the said Governor and Com-"pany." It is clear from this language that Parliament understood by "banking" only the issue of notes, and that the exclusive privilege of the Bank did not prevent the issue of such notes by partnerships having only six partners or less, nor the performance of the other banking functions by companies or partnerships of a greater number of partners. Notes were accordingly issued by the London private banking houses, some of which were of longer standing than the Bank of England itself, and by country bankers, of whom the number increased rapidly in the second half of the eighteenth century.*

The London bankers, it is true, began not far from the year 1772 to discontinue the issue of notes, finding the check system identical in its advantages and more convenient in practice ; but their right of issue was merely in abeyance, until it was formally taken away in 1844. The country bankers, however, with many vicissitudes of fortune, have continued the issue of notes to this day, subject to the restrictions contained in the Bank Charter Act of 1844, presently to be described.

That the Bank monopoly in its strict interpretation also permitted the exercise of all banking functions, except issue,

---

* McLeod's Dictionary of Political Economy, p. 89. In his *Theory and Practice of Banking*, I, 211, Mr. McLeod says that the latest London banker's note preserved is dated 1793.

by joint stock banks and companies of more than six persons, had indeed been noticed, but seems to have been little considered, until the discussions of 1826, renewed upon the revision of the charter in 1833. The growing demands of the country for banking facilities and the slowness with which the Bank of England responded to these demands by the establishment of branches, caused much unsound banking by private firms, while a lingering doubt as to the meaning of the monopoly prevented the foundation of joint-stock banks with large capital. Lord Liverpool is reported as declaring in 1826, that the effect of the law "is to permit every description of banking, except that which is solid and secure." The result of this state of things was that, notwithstanding the resistance of the Bank of England, an important exception was made to the monopoly enjoyed by the Bank. An act passed in 1826, gave to companies of more than six persons the right of issuing notes, when established at a greater distance than sixty-five miles from London; and the act of 1833 for renewing the charter, expressly declared that companies and partnerships, although composed of more than six persons, might carry on the business of banking in London, or within the radius of sixty-five miles, provided they should issue no circulating notes.*

This legislation was followed by a great extension of joint-stock banking. The London and Westminster Joint-Stock Bank, now the largest bank of deposit in existence, was established the next year,† and many banks of issue began business outside the geographical limit. The extension, however, was too rapid to be sound; the disturbed condition

---

* 7 *George* IV., ch. 46; 3 *and* 4 *William* IV., ch. 98.

† The London and Westminster was for many years under the management of James W. Gilbart, author of several works on banking, and owes its existence largely to his sagacity. For a short account of its early struggles, see Gilbart, *Principles and Practice of Banking*, 462.

of business affairs for a large part of the next decade stimulated agitation; and the general opinion found in a vicious note circulation the cause of the repeated commercial crises. The necessity for a renewal of the charter of the Bank of England in 1844 gave to the government of Sir Robert Peel an opportunity both for revising the organization of the Bank, and for putting an end to the increase of their issues by the joint-stock banks, and the result was the passage of the measure known as the "Bank Charter Act of 1844," or "Peel's Act," in which are embodied the leading provisions by which the bank-note circulation of England and Wales is now regulated.* By this act, Parliament undertook to make the notes of the Bank of England secure, and to limit the issue of bank-notes of all other kinds in England and Wales.

3. To accomplish the first of these objects the act provided for the division of the Bank into two departments, the Issue Department and the Banking Department. The former was charged exclusively with the issue and redemption of notes; the latter was restricted to the ordinary business of discount and deposit; and in all dealings with each other the two departments were made as independent as if they belonged to distinct corporations. For all notes issued by it the Issue Department was required to hold either government securities, or coin or bullion; and the amount of securities which it could hold being limited by the original provision to £14,000,000, it followed that for all notes outstanding in excess of that amount it must have an equivalent in the precious metals.† As experience

---

* 7 and 8 *Victoria*, ch. 32. For abstracts of this important act, see McCulloch, *Commercial Dictionary* (edition of 1857), 84; Gilbart, *Principles and Practice of Banking*, 428; Fenn, *Compendium of the Funds*, (ed. 1883) 77.

† The act provides that of the coin and bullion held by the Issue Department one-fifth may be silver. For the reason for this provision see *Hansard's Debates*, May 20, 1844, p. 1334. The bank ceased to hold silver for this purpose in September, 1853.

had shown that the ordinary uses of the country never failed to require an amount of notes higher than £14,000,000, this provision insured the presence of coin or bullion for the redemption of all notes whose presentation for payment could be deemed morally possible, and made it unnecessary to fix any limit to the issue. The ordinary business of the Issue Department was then reduced to the automatic function of giving out notes for coin, or coin for notes,* as the public might demand.

Under this arrangement the Banking Department carries on its business of buying securities and using its credit in the form of deposits, on the same general principles on which any bank of deposit and discount is conducted. It is bound to meet all its demand liabilities in cash, and for this purpose it habitually maintains a reserve, consisting either of specie or of notes convertible into specie by the Issue Department. It is bound to make its payments in gold, if so required, like other banks; but it may make payment in notes with the consent of the payee; and if, for the convenience of its customers, it finds occasion to pay out a greater amount of notes than it receives in payments made to it, or in deposits, it must procure such notes, as any other bank or any private person must, by taking an equivalent amount of gold to the Issue Department and procuring notes therefor. Indeed, so completely is the Banking Department deprived of all special facilities or privileges in dealing with the Issue Department, that it has often been said that for all practical purposes the notes might

---

* The Issue Department is also made an intermediary between the public and the Mint, being required to buy all gold bullion offered at 77s. 9d. per standard ounce. The ounce is coined into 77s. 10½d., the difference being the estimated equivalent for a loss of interest, caused by the delay incident to the actual coining at the Mint. *Hankey on Banking*, 98.

as well be issued by a public office at Westminster as by a department of the Bank itself.*

The second purpose of Peel's Act is accomplished by a series of provisions which prevent any increase of the note issues of joint-stock and private banks beyond the average at which they stood for the twelve weeks preceding April 27, 1844. No bank not then engaged in the issue of notes is allowed to issue them, and no bank then existing can carry its issue beyond the limit thus fixed for it. It is provided, however, that if any bank issuing notes at the time when the act was passed, shall close its business, or become bankrupt, or discontinue its issues by agreement with the Bank of England or otherwise, then the latter may add to the amount of securities held in its Issue Department, or in other words to the amount of notes for which it holds securities and not coin, to the extent of two-thirds of the amount of joint-stock or private banknotes thus withdrawn from circulation. The act then plainly looks forward to the complete withdrawal of all other notes than those of the Bank of England, and to the filling of the vacant place by the latter, in a certain measure. No new issues being permitted, every change, however brought about, diminishes the amount of country banknotes left in use. The progress towards extinction is probably slower than was expected. Still, since 1844 the authorized country bank issue has been reduced, by the winding up of

---

* In Ricardo's pamphlet, *A Plan for a National Bank*, *Works*, 499, it is proposed that the notes should be issued to the Bank by public commissioners, holding securities and gold substantially as at present. This pamphlet, left in MS. at Ricardo's death and first published in 1824, is the first distinct proposition which we now recollect for the separation of the issue and banking departments. Public discussion of the subject seems to have begun as early as 1837. The suggestion that the separation was suggested by the New York free banking system is certainly without foundation. *Old and New*, VIII. 590.

banks or by the surrender of the right, from £8,648,853 to £5,854,502, and the Bank of England has added, under the authority of the act, to its own issues covered by securities only, until the limit has risen to £15,750,000. But it is plainly not the policy of this legislation that there should ever be a large circulation of banknotes. The smallest note issued by the Bank, indeed the smallest lawfully issued by any authority since 1829, is for £5, a denomination too large to make its way far from cities and large towns, and of but limited use even in those places.* A large circulation of sovereigns, affording a solid basis of specie in the hands of the people, with a small amount of convertible notes for convenient use in some large transactions, is the ideal condition towards which the uniform current of English law has now pointed for nearly fifty years.

4. To illustrate more clearly the operation of the act we will take the account of the Bank as it stood September 7, 1844, being the account on which the act first took effect. The situation of the Bank at that date was as follows :—

Liabilities.			*Resources.*	
Capital	£14.6		Government Debt	£11.
Rest	3.6		" Securities	17.6
Public Deposits	3.6		Other Securities	7.8
Other "	8.6		Coin and Bullion	15.2
Seven-day bills	1.			
Notes	20.2			
	51.6			51.6

---

* The Bank of England issued no notes so small as £5 until 1759. See *ante* p. 65. In 1797, after the suspension of specie payment it was authorized to issue notes as small as £1, but withdrew them after the return to specie payments. It made a temporary issue of them at the end of 1825 and in 1826, but these also were withdrawn before 1829, in conformity with an act passed in 1826. The issue of £1 notes by country bankers was forbidden as early as 1777, but was permitted from 1797 to 1829.

As no attempt was made by law to protect by preference any special class of liabilities, before the passage of Peel's Act, it follows that the resources set down in this statement* were held equally for notes and deposits; and it is at least conceivable that there might be so strong a demand for coin by depositors as to exhaust the reserve, while a large issue of notes was still outstanding, in which case payment of the notes must be suspended. Thus in the frightful panic of December, 1825, the coin and bullion of the Bank was reduced to £1,027,000 and suspension was imminent, while notes were still outstanding to the amount of £23,359,840. Such a possibility became still more serious after the act of 1833 declared that the notes of the bank, so long as they continued to be redeemed on presentation, should be a legal tender in England and Wales in all payments except those at the Bank itself. It was, therefore, an important object, in separating the departments, to insure the payment of the notes in any event, by pledging for that purpose a sufficient amount of securities and of specie.† How this result was accomplished is easily seen in

---

* In the Bank of England statements, Rest (*i. e.* the balance of the account) means the net profits on hand; other deposits is synonymous with individual deposits and deposits by banks; Seven-day bills are past-notes, still issued to a small amount; Government Debt is the loan made by the Bank to the government, in order to secure its charter; and other securities includes loans and advances to customers upon security.

† Whether in case of the insolvency of the Bank the securities and specie in the issue department would be held for the preferred claim of the notes, or would become a part of the general assets, to be divided among all the creditors, is not explicitly declared by the act and has been doubted. But it has no doubt been the common understanding from the first that the devotion of the resources of the Issue Department to the payment of its notes is indefeasible. See *Parliamentary Documents, 1857–58*, V. 427.

the form of statement of the Bank account, adopted upon the passage of the act, and ever since adhered to:

Issue Department.

Notes . . .	£20.2	Government debt . . .	£11.
		Other government securities	3.
		Coin and bullion . . .	6.2
	£20.2		£20.2

Banking Department.

Capital	14.6	Government securities	14.6
Rest	3.6	Other securities . . .	7.8
Public deposits .	3.6	Notes* . , ...	
Other "	8.6	Coin and bullion . . .	9.
Seven-day bills .	1.		
	31.4		31.4

The thoroughness of the provision here made for the security of the banknote is attested by the fact that since the passage of the act there has never been a moment when the convertibility of the note has even been open to doubt. The lowest point to which the notes outstanding have ever been reduced was a little below £17,000,000 in December, 1848, and this left in the vaults of the Issue Department nearly £14,000,000 in specie, with no demand for it on the part of the public. Indeed, the Bank of England note, under the act of 1844, has become little more than a warrant entitling the holder to so much gold actually lying in the Bank vaults, and thus the whole question as to

---

* The above shows the effect of the separation of accounts taken by itself. For convenience the Banking Department also transferred 8.2 millions of coin and bullion to the Issue Department and received notes therefor, so that in the published accounts the banking reserve was 8.2 millions of notes and .8 millions of coin, and both the notes and the coin and bullion in the accounts of the Issue Department were raised by 8.2 millions.

the solvency of the paper currency has been removed from the field of debate where it had been agitated for so many years. The Issue Department gains nothing from an increase of the circulation, and can lose nothing by its diminution. The whole problem as to the banknote is reduced to a mere inquiry as to the preference of the public for coin or for a certificate calling for coin.

It is evident also that to the Banking Department it is of no consequence, except as regards convenience, whether it uses notes or gold in its business. If it prefers gold it has only to send in for redemption such notes as it holds or receives in the course of its business; if it prefers notes it has only to send in its gold for exchange. Its reserve is in fact composed like that of any other bank, of gold or of notes which are good for gold, or of both; and this reserve it must procure in the first instance, must maintain, and in case of need must replenish, as any other bank must, by properly adjusting its purchases of securities. Its profits would obviously be the same as now if it discontinued the use of the notes altogether, except so far as they might be affected by the mere inconvenience of dealing, already referred to. Indeed, nearly the whole income of the Bank of England, beyond the simple return on the investment of its capital, is derived from the use of its credit in the form of deposits in the Banking Department. So far as concerns the other form of demand liability, the notes, the only profit possible under the act of 1844 is limited to the interest received on the £15,750,000 of securities. This interest is now offset by payments to the government and other charges to such an extent that the question has been raised seriously, whether it would not be for the advantage of the stockholders if the Bank were relieved from all connection with the issue of notes.*

---

* The annual profit on the issue of notes is estimated by Mr. Hankey at less than £100,000. *Hankey on Banking* (3rd ed.) p. 63.

5. Complete as is the separation between the departments in theory, and generally even in fact, it has nevertheless happened several times, under the exceptional conditions of a financial crisis, that the embarrassments of the Banking Department have affected the issue of notes in a manner not originally contemplated by the framers of the act. On three occasions it has been found necessary to disregard that provision which limits the securities held by the Issue Department, and more than once this extreme measure has been only narrowly escaped.* In order to understand the real significance of these occurrences, it is necessary to take into consideration the circumstances under which the Bank of England holds its banking reserve.

The most striking fact in the situation of the Bank of England is that the Bank is the centre of a great system of joint stock and private banks, whose business and whose liabilities are many times greater than its own, and that to this system of banks are confided the financial affairs of the city which may almost be said to be the Clearing House of the world. It is at all events true that many of the largest trades in the world make their settlement in London, and that especially the world's supply of gold there finds its natural point of distribution. From this it would follow, even if England were not herself a great lender of capital, that many of the operations of lending and paying undertaken by others must be carried on through London. The banks through which a cosmopolitan business of this kind passes must at times find themselves subject to great and sudden demands. The nature of their liabilities is not constant; it varies with every

---

* The limiting clause of the act of 1844 was disregarded, or, as is commonly said, "suspended," October 25, 1847, November 12, 1857, and May 12, 1866. In February, 1861, and in May and September, 1864, the condition of things was critical; and in November, 1873, the suspension of the act appeared for some days not improbable.

change in the condition of any foreign country of importance, and is at one time steady, and at another time uncertain. The reserves, therefore, which are at one time adequate for the protection of these liabilities, are at another time too small. These reserves, however, which belong to the individual members of the great system of banks, are not held in practice by the banks themselves. The London banks, from long habit, keep their chief reserves as private persons might, deposited in the Bank of England, retaining in their own hands only such small amounts as are needed for the demands of the moment, and drawing upon the Bank for more important sums. Of the "other deposits" of the Bank of England a large part represents the liability of the Bank to its neighbors incurred in this manner.*

The position of the Bank of England, then, is not simply that of a bank whose deposits are liable to serious fluctuations of a peculiar nature; it is also a position of great responsibility. Whether by its own action or by the force of circumstances the Bank holds in its charge that on which the solvency of the banks in general, the safety of the commercial public, and the credit of England alike depend. Its managers have sometimes proposed to regard it as simply a bank carried on for the profit of its own stockholders; but so long as it holds the banking deposits it has in its hands the financial safety of the whole community, the real leadership of the money-market, and cannot escape its accountability for the manner in which it performs the duties of its position. As regards the issue of notes its duties are too plain and even mechanical to throw upon it any serious burden of this kind, but as the depository of the other banks it is in effect charged with the duty of providing for all.

---

* Dun, *British Banking Statistics*, 124; Bagehot, *Lombard Street*, 307. In 1877 the bankers' deposits in the Bank of England were reported as varying for £13.3 millions in January to £8 millions in May. *Parliamentary Documents*, 1878, XLVI.

In this respect, as holding a reserve wherewith to repay the borrowed reserves of others, the Bank of England, as has been said, holds a position remarkably similar to that of the banks of New York city, with the difference, however, that its responsibility for prudent management is undivided and, therefore, inevitable. Of course, the position would be one of perfect safety if the Banking Department regularly held cash for all its banking liabilities,—that is, either coin or notes redeemable in coin by the Issue Department. Its sources of profit being the same, however, as those of other banks, the Banking Department finds its interest as they do, in the conversion of idle cash into interest-bearing securities, so far as possible, and in holding, therefore, no larger cash reserve than is required for safety. Acting on its reserve by raising or lowering its rate of discount,* it is under a great temptation to defer as long as possible the diminution of its business by the raising of its rate, and may thus be led to keep itself weak down to the moment when it needs to be strong. And it may happen, moreover, that the reserve, being suddenly reduced by causes not to be foreseen, cannot be raised by the slow action of the rate of discount in time to escape all the consequences of such a misfortune. In every case of remarkable pressure which has occurred since the separation of the two departments, and in most of those which happened before, the real difficulty presented will be found to have been that of meeting liabilities for deposits with a reserve which had become insufficient, either from continued negligence in the past, or from sudden demands on a great scale.† Of these cases we will take

---

* Until 1833 the usury laws had led the Bank to adhere to a uniform rate of discount. The present system of a sliding scale was not fairly adopted before 1839.

† That the Bank, as an important and usually well informed leader, may lead the market, but cannot control it at pleasure by changes of rate, see Bagehot's *Lombard Street*, 114.

THE BANK OF ENGLAND. 79

for examination, as an illustration of the present topic, the narrow escape of the Bank in the great commercial crisis of November, 1857, a case which may fairly be regarded as typical.

6. There is no doubt that in England the materials for this crisis had been long in preparation. Rapid commercial expansion and a great extension of credit had brought the usual results in the form of unsound business, of speculative prices and of extreme sensitiveness to any threatening influence. If no sudden pressure had occurred all might have passed off in a mere subsidence of activity and in general depression; but the sudden occurrence of a disastrous revulsion in the United States, bringing ruin to some and carrying apprehension to all, developed a panic which took the whole community by surprise. In August the state of things was reputed to be "not unsatisfactory"; no fear seems to have been felt until the middle of September, when heavy failures in New York, beginning with that of the Ohio Life Insurance and Trust Company on the 24th of August, became known in London. Still, although gold began to leave England for the continent, and the pressure in New York had caused the cessation of specie exports to England, the directors of the Bank of England seem not to have thought the difficulty serious. It was not until October 8th, when the news of the suspension of payments by the banks of Philadelphia and Baltimore proved that something more than an ordinary embarrassment existed, that they determined to raise their rate of discount, from the point at which it had stood since July 16, to six per cent. At this point the condition of the Bank was disquieting. In the course of three weeks it had materially increased its loans, but was losing seriously from its reserve, so that the proportion of reserve to liabilities had changed much for the worse, at a time when general uneasiness was beginning to make the commercial public more than ever anxious to borrow, as a prudent provision for the uncertainties of the immediate future. It

may fairly be said then, we believe, that a singular tardiness of action on the part of the Bank was the immediate cause of much that ensued.

Without following the steps by which the crisis from this point was converted into panic, we will take the state of things existing in the early days of November, when the Bank rate stood at eight per cent. At this juncture the alarm caused by the failure of several large firms and of one or two provincial banks of some importance had intensified the demand for loans, both upon the Bank of England and the other banks in the city. The increasing disposition of the latter to strengthen their own position, in view of the possible heavy demands to which their great liabilities exposed them, not only threw much of the increased pressure for loans upon the Bank of England, but also led to a marked increase in the bankers' balances, that is in the deposits of reserve by other banks. At the same time with this serious change in the amount and character of the liabilities, the cash resources of the Bank were falling. An active export of specie to the United States had taken a considerable amount from the reserve, the rise of rates on the continent of Europe had made it impossible to draw specie from that quarter, while the apprehension of banks in the interior led to a serious absorption of cash by them. In short, at a time when it was called upon to extend its use of its own credit, the Bank found itself acted upon by what has been called an internal drain as well as an external one.

The bank met this dilemma by raising its rate of discount on the 5th to nine per cent., in the hope of repelling the least necessitous borrowers, and by making in the course of the next week an increase of loans to the amount of three millions and a half. Before the end of the week, however, the state of affairs had become desperate. The general alarm had deepened with the rapid succession of failures in the commercial world and the suspension of the great Western Bank

THE BANK OF ENGLAND. 81

of Scotland*; the moderate increase of loans by the Bank of England had done nothing towards quieting the public; some sales of securities had been effected by the Bank, but the drain upon its reserve as well as the increasing liability for bankers' deposits continued. The rate of discount was raised on the 9th to ten per cent. but without avail. The joint-stock banks and private bankers had finally ceased discounting, so that from Monday, the 9th, the whole demand for loans was thrown upon the Bank of England, whose reserve on the 11th had fallen to little more than one-tenth of its "other deposits." On that day came the suspension of the City of Glasgow Bank,† caused by the general alarm created by the failure of the Western Bank; other banks called for assistance; and a great discounting firm in the city failed on the same day. In four days, beginning with the 9th, the Bank advanced to the public over five millions sterling, but without the effect of subduing the panic or stopping the drain of its reserve, and on the evening of the 12th it found itself with a liability for deposits amounting to thirteen millions, and a reserve of cash in its banking department of only £581,000,‡ an amount which the single check of more than one depositor might exhaust. Unless some change beyond all hope should occur, this feeble reserve might be expected to disappear long before the close of the next day.

In all this there had been nothing resembling a run upon the Issue Department. Gold required for export or for the interior was indeed drawn ultimately from that department, for it was provided by those who were directly or indirectly

---

* The ruin of this bank, which in 1857 discounted to the amount of £20,000,000 and had deposits of £6,500,000, was precipitated by losses in America, although not strictly caused by them.

† The final and disastrous failure of this bank in October, 1878, will long be remembered.

‡ Of this only £384,000 was in London, the remainder being held by the branches of the Bank.

creditors of the Banking Department, who drew therefore from the banking reserve and thus caused notes held in that reserve to be presented to the Issue Department for redemption. But the gold was not obtained by the presentation of notes hitherto in circulation or held outside of the Bank, for from the 10th of October to the 11th of November, the amount of notes thus in the hands of the public is shown by the account to have been almost without change. What had occurred was that the Banking Department had been caught at the beginning of a severe pressure with an insufficient banking reserve and had been slow in taking measures for escape. The position of the Bank was such as that of the London and Westminster Bank might have been, had its reserve of cash run down while its liability was large, except that the latter had no chain of dependent banks. It was a case of near approach to failure, as simple in its essentials as that of any private banker who is unable to meet his depositors, or any incorporated bank which is not a bank of issue and meets with similar misfortune.

Under ordinary circumstances a ready means of replenishing the reserve might be found in the sale of securities for cash, and such a course, it has been suggested, would be taken by the Bank of England in a case like the present. This resource can be used, however, at the height of a crisis, only to a moderate extent. Buyers, even of the soundest securities, are at such a time few and reluctant, partly because of the universal disposition to keep a firm hold upon cash as the safest provision for an unknown future, and partly because of the prospect that low prices may be succeeded by still lower. Moreover it is to be remembered that purchases to any considerable extent would have to be made by those holders of capital who have their funds deposited either with the joint-stock or private banks, or with the Bank of England itself; and in either case the check given in payment for securities would finally be a demand upon the Bank of England itself by one of its depositors. The sale of securities would then serve to extinguish a part of the liabilities, and to that extent would improve the condition of the Bank, but it would bring in no cash to meet the steady drain upon the reserve.*

7. The Bank, then, on the 12th of November, reached the end of its tether. Following the precedent of the year 1847, therefore, the management informed the government of the critical condition in which they stood, and received in return a virtual authority for the issue by the Issue Department of a further amount of notes secured by government securities.† Thus empowered, the Banking Department transferred to the Issue Department securities to the amount of two millions, and in exchange therefor received notes which were placed in the reserve. The operation was in effect a sale of securities to the Issue Department, in default of other purchasers, and the receipt of payment in notes, redeemable on presentation. The effect on the Issue Department was to increase the absolute amount as well as the proportion of the notes issued by it upon securities instead of coin or bullion, but the notes did not for that reason cease to be redeemable or to be redeemed in the regular course of daily business. Carried to a great extent the operation might plainly have weakened the notes by endangering their convertibility. Restricted as it was, however, it cannot

---

* On the possibility of a sale of securities on a large scale during a panic, see Bagehot's *Lombard Street*, 190.

† This practical setting aside of an act of Parliament was in the form of an assurance that, if the Bank found it necessary to take the step proposed, the ministry would ask Parliament to indemnify them for any consequences of such illegal action. Besides the publication of the entire correspondence in the Parliamentary documents, which has been made on every occasion of the suspension of the Bank Act, the "government letter" is given by the *Economist* of November 14, 1857, and all the correspondence for 1866 in the *Annual Register* of that year, p. 305.

be said to have had any real influence on the strength of the note issue, the credit of which remained unimpaired from the beginning to the end of the crisis. The effect on the Banking Department was to give it an immediate accession of means to the amount of two millions, with the assurance that more could be had if needed, the only discernible limit to the relief being the conceivable inability of the Issue Department to continue the redemption of an indefinitely enlarged issue of notes, —a theoretical limit too distant to have any practical bearing.

The assistance given to the Banking Department did not consist so much in the actual addition of cash to its resources, as in the quieting effect of the measure on the public mind. In every such state of affairs it is a factor of prime consequence that much of the public excitement is pure panic,—an unreasoning terror, which multiplies danger by destroying presence of mind. For the easy movement of business under the credit system confidence in each other and in the future is necessary. The producer or merchant, using borrowed capital, relies upon the sale of goods and upon fresh loans for the means of repaying former advances, and if the current is interrupted, if doubt on the part of buyers prevents sales, or embarrassment of lenders prevents or diminishes loans, the fears of debtors, to whom the failure to obtain the means of making their payments when due means bankruptcy and ruin, become at times ungovernable. No man is any longer sure of anything except his own indebtedness and its near maturity; there is a universal pressure to borrow, even beyond the real needs of the moment, lest borrowing should presently become impossible; and there is a universal tightening of the grasp on all ready means by such as are so fortunate as to have them. The *sauve qui peut* of merchants, become desperate as to their means of payment, is as mutually destructive and as fatal to their hopes of escape, as is the crush of a panic-stricken audience, blocking the exit from a burning building.

THE BANK OF ENGLAND. 85

To a community thus dominated by universal terror, the Bank of England was able to say that its potential reserve now fixed no limit to its ability to extend its loans and meet all consequent liabilities. The effect of this assurance in allaying the panic was instantaneous. Men ceased to press for what might not be needed after all, and the other banks in the city, no longer dreading demands from their own depositors, resumed their operations. Confidence had indeed suffered too severe a shock to recover without that process of liquidation which is called a revulsion of business; but the liquidation, instead of being immediate, could now be gradual enough to enable debtors to collect and realize upon their resources with some deliberation.

It was not then so much the four millions which the Bank felt safe in adding to its securities in a week after the suspension of the act of 1844, as the moral relief given to the public, which constituted the real remedy by which the crisis was ended. As for the change in the amount of the note issues of the Bank, we may fairly deny that in itself it had any influence whatever, so trifling was its amount. The notes issued in excess of the statutory limit, and actually in the hands of the public, stood at their highest point on the 20th of November, when they amounted to £928,000, and by the end of the month the Issue Department had returned to its normal condition.* Indeed the difference between the minimum and maximum of the outstanding notes for the month was only £1,300,000.

8. The conditions on which this singular abandonment of the terms of the Bank charter has been allowed are jealously

---

* This opinion that the relief given by the suspension of the limit fixed by the act is a moral relief and is not to be found in the actual issue of notes, is confirmed by the fact that neither in October, 1847, nor in May, 1866, was the issue of notes upon securities increased at all, —the mere announcement that such issue would be made, if needed for the reserve, being sufficient to quell the panic.

guarded. The Bank has been required to pay over to the government all profits made by it from any increase of issues above the statutory limit, and both in 1857 and 1866 it was required to maintain its rate of discount at ten per cent., so long as it should use the permission given to it. As this rate would have for its effect to drive away business from the Bank as soon as the rate in the general market should fall, the condition insures as speedy a return to the legal limit of the issue as is practicable.

Whatever the conditions, however, the repeated resort to this extra-legal measure, and the public confidence that it will always be resorted to in like case, are a remarkable derogation from an elaborate scheme of legislation and the substitution of a roughly improvised expedient, for which it would be difficult to find a parallel, even in English administration. And the question has been raised with good reason as to the real value of a legal limit which is to be set aside when it begins to press. Why not, it is said, allow the Issue Department to keep such amount of securities as is found advisable, always holding it to the duty and the test of instant redemption? No doubt, if the provisions of the act of 1844 were to be defended solely on the grounds on which they were originally urged by Sir Robert Peel, they would have to be condemned. He expected the act to prove a remedy for financial crises; whereas, not only have such crises recurred with the same rough periodicity since the passage of the act as before it, but they are probably sharper in the London market by reason of the very existence of the act which was to cure them. The act has, however, served the purpose of making the legal tender paper of England safe and convertible in every contingency which is even remotely possible. It has rendered an even greater service, while thus eliminating the question of convertibility, by setting in its true light, as the kernel of all banking problems, the question as to the proper management of the banking reserve. No such mistakes of management could now occur as marked the whole course of the history of the Bank in the first half of the century. The Bank was not quick to learn the real risks of its position and its responsibilities; but still it has learned them, and now guards its reserve with vigilance, by appropriate means, and with general success. It takes the alarm sooner than formerly, it sets its customary line of supposed safety higher, and thus in a great catastrophe like that of 1873 it escaped the disaster which befell it, in a condition of affairs not more dangerous, in 1857. Whether the provisions of law which have effected these improvements are perfect may be doubted.* Probably an elastic provision like that contained in the German legislation would be easier in operation and equally effectual. But some provision other than that suggested by the temporary policy or interest of the Bank itself the law cannot fail to make, in a system of banking and currency so highly concentrated as that which England has long maintained.

9. From what has been said it will be seen that the Bank of England, although a highly privileged establishment, is not a government institution. It has a partial monopoly of the right of issuing notes, which in theory is destined to become complete; it has the distinction of having its notes the only paper legal tender in the United Kingdom; it is the chief depository of a government which maintains no public Treasury; it is charged with the duty of keeping the registry of the public debt and of paying the interest thereon; still it is a private corporation of the familiar type, managed by its own officers, in whose selection the government has no share, and whose responsibility is to their own stockholders alone. The Bank has duties thrown upon it, partly by laws and partly by force of circumstances, which make it a highly important member of

---

* For Mr. Lowe's bill to authorize the suspension of the limit of 1844, under fixed regulations, see *Economist* for 1873, pp. 741, 748.

the body politic, and yet it is in form a corporation intended to earn dividends for the owners of its stock. For many years after its foundation it was even forbidden by law to lend to the government beyond a certain narrow limit without the express sanction of Parliament,* and although it has now for a long time been a trusted agent and has at times compromised its own safety by its financial support of the exchequer, it has never failed in its dealings with the authorities to assert its own essential independence.

The organization of the Bank is as anomalous as its position. It is governed by twenty-four directors, custom making bankers ineligible to that position, and by a Governor and Deputy Governor. The directors are elected annually, and by usage a part of the board is changed every year; but the changes take place among the younger members, so that after some years of possibly intermittent service, the director's tenure of his position is practically for life. After many years he usually becomes Deputy Governor for two years, in due rotation, and then Governor for the like term, after which and for the remainder of his official life he is a member of an executive council of directors known as the Committee of Treasury. The director enters upon office, therefore, at an early age and reaches the positions of most active responsibility only after a long training in the Bank itself. Such an organization would hardly be proposed if the case were new, but it is, no doubt, well fitted, indeed too well fitted, to preserve the traditions of policy and of management which secure the Bank from rapid change.†

Under a direction thus organized the Bank has now enjoyed a long course of prosperity, seldom interrupted for any length of time. Its imprudent loans to the government early

---

* This prohibition continued until the year 1793.

† On the government of the Bank, see Bagehot, *Lombard Street*, ch. viii.

in the wars of the French revolution caused its long suspension of specie payment, from February, 1797 to May, 1821, but the Bank reaped a rich harvest from its issue of irredeemable paper.* In the crisis of December, 1825, it was on the point of failure, and in 1838 and 1839 it was forced to obtain material aid from the Bank of France. Still, since 1852, its dividends have never been at a less rate than 8 per cent. for any one year, and have averaged $9\frac{1}{2}$ per cent. since 1870. The stock has not been lower in price than 156 per cent. since 1840, has for thirty-five years steadily kept above 200, and for much of the time since the early part of 1883 has stood well above 300.

---

* For a statement of the dividends and bonuses received by the stockholders from 1797 to 1816, together with a searching inquiry into the profits made by the Bank from its relations with the government, see Ricardo's pamphlet, *Proposals for an Economical and Secure Currency*, especially the table, *Works*, p. 427.

CHAPTER VII.

THE BANK OF FRANCE.

1. FROM 1793 to the latter part of 1796, banking can hardly be said to have existed in France. The government tolerated no issue of paper except its own; the Caisse d'Escompte, which appears to have been the only public bank for several years, had been suppressed, and the times were too disturbed for private banking to flourish. With the disappearance from circulation of the *assignats*, and of their successors, the *mandats territoriaux*, the issue of notes appears to have become again a matter of common right, to be undertaken by anybody who could gain the confidence of the public; and accordingly a bank of issue called the Caisse des Comptes Courants was organized in Paris in the last half of 1796, and began its operations with fair success. Two others of some importance were established by the year 1800, besides some smaller ones of which little is now known; and in Rouen a bank of discount and issue was in active business as early as 1798.

The Bank of France was also established in Paris in 1800, under the encouragement of the government and with the First Consul as a stockholder, but upon a footing not essentially different from that of its neighbors. Its capital of 30,000,000 francs was the largest yet proposed and the difficulty of raising it led to a fusion with the Caisse des Comptes Courants, but no monopoly was created. One public bureau, holding a large amount of funds, was required to invest them in shares of the new bank, and large deposits were made in it by the government; still, although favored, the Bank of France stood legally upon an equality with the rest and nothing more.* So far it might be said that the field was open in France for a wide and free diffusion of banking facilities, and that a beginning had been made.

In 1803, however, Napoleon announced a complete change of policy and the Bank of France was thereupon made the sole bank of issue, its capital was raised to 45,000,000 francs, and its charter extended to 1818.† All other issues of notes were at once withdrawn, one of the rival banks in Paris was absorbed by the rising monopoly, and another assumed for a time the humble place of intermediary between the great bank and its less important customers. No provincial bank could thereafter be established without the authority of the government. Under this arrangement, and notwithstanding the provision that no notes should be issued in Paris for less than 500 francs, the circulation of the Bank rapidly increased with its expanding discounts. It is plain in fact that the strong preference of the public for bank credit in the form of notes left but a narrow field for those banks which could only open deposit accounts, and justified the government in its opinion of the importance then to be attached to the right of emission. And the fact that in the existing state of things, with the existing habits of business, the credit in the form of notes was so strongly preferred, gave to the monopoly of the Bank an influence on the future history of banking in France far beyond that which a

---

* Courtois, *Histoire des Banques en France*, 108–112. The articles of association, containing the statutes of the Bank, adopted by the shareholders at the start, are in the *Moniteur*, 5 Pluv. VIII., (25 January, 1800).

† The law of 24 Germinal XI. (14 April, 1803) and most of the subsequent legislation concerning the Bank down to 1857 is given in Wolowski, *La Question des Banques*, 425. The Statutes of the Bank of 1803 are in the *Moniteur*, 15 Brumaire, XII. (7 November, 1803).

similar monopoly could have exercised in the same years in England.*

Although the Bank of France still chose its own officers and enjoyed a nominal independence, it was now becoming involved in the bold operations of the French Treasury. Complications thus arising reduced the cash in the Bank in the latter part of 1805 so far that it was found necessary to limit the redemption of notes to 600,000 francs daily, until such time as specie could be collected in sufficient quantity for complete resumption. The result of this crisis, however, was not to separate the Bank from the government, but to connect them still more closely; and in the spring of 1806 a measure was therefore adopted which definitely settled the character of the Bank as a public institution. By the doubling of its capital and the extension of its privileges to 1843,† not only its preeminence in the financial world of France, but its absolute importance, was assured, so far as it depended on legislation; and its direction, hitherto confided to a board of regents chosen by the stockholders, was transferred to a governor and two sub-governors, to be nominated by the chief of the State. Under a government not inclined to use power for its own ends, this species of control might for the time become a mere trusteeship on the part of the State; under an Emperor like Napoleon it made the bank an engine of the State,—a private corporation, indeed, as regards the legal ownership of its property, but a public office as regards the actual employment of the property. Successive governments in France have used this opportunity in different ways as the case has seemed to require; but such as Napoleon made the Bank in 1806 it has remained ever since,

---

* That the government was actively hostile to the other banks of circulation, see Courcelle-Seneuil, *Traité des Opérations de Banque*, 217.

† In 1840 the privilege was extended to 1867, and in 1857 was further extended to 1897.

THE BANK OF FRANCE.

an institution subject to the control, and therefore subservient to the needs of the government of the day.*

2. In the closing years of the Empire the altered constitution of the Bank made itself felt in the great increase of transactions with the Treasury, which became more and more compromising and finally far exceeded in amount the advances made to the commercial public. When, therefore, France was invaded by the allies in the winter of 1813-14, a run by the noteholders began, caused, it is probable, chiefly by the fact that the bank appeared to have no independent existence of its own, and it again became necessary for three months to limit the amount of the daily redemption of notes to 500,000 francs. Full payment was resumed in April, 1814, but the settlement of the affairs of the Bank was pushed on both sides, until its loans were reduced to less than 3,000,000 francs, and its circulation had fallen from 95,000,000 francs to 15,700,000.† The enlarged capital of the Bank had been found, even in the latter years of Napoleon's reign, to be larger than could be used with profit, and the Bank had therefore, as early as 1812, made large purchases of its own stock. These were continued in 1816, until the capital was reduced to 67,900 francs, at which point it remained until 1848. Lafitte, who became governor of the Bank under the Restoration, desired to improve the opportunity for general change, by setting the institution free from the control of the government, and bringing it back to

---

* The Statutes of the Bank, under the law of April 22, 1806, were established by the Emperor, January 16, 1808. See Wolowski as above, and *Moniteur*, January 18, 1808. In Block's *Dictionnaire de l'Administration*, is a detailed account of the organization and operations of the Bank.

† The *Moniteur* for January 31, 1815, contains a report by Lafitte, then provisional governer of the Bank, giving in some detail the operations for the year 1814. For tables giving the leading figures of the account of the Bank from 1800 to 1879, see Courtois, *Histoire*, 344, 360.

the safe position of a genuine bank of discount; but, although his views appear to have been supported by the ministry, no measure for carrying them out could be passed and the imperial decree of 1808, strengthened as we shall see by the action of the Republic in 1848, has continued to be the working constitution of the Bank.

The government of the Restoration appears, however, to have adopted the policy of restricting the monopoly of the Bank to the capital. An imperial decree of 1808 had authorized the Bank to establish branches (*comptoirs d'escompte*) with the right of issue, subject to governmental approval, plainly with the design of centralizing the banking interests of the empire under the lead of the great Bank in Paris.* Under this decree the establishment of branches in Lyons and Lille was undertaken, although with little success, and one was set in operation at Rouen. The Bourbon government in 1817 and 1818 closed these branches and established independent banks at Rouen, Nantes, and Bordeaux, giving to them the right of emission, and thus reversing the policy of Napoleon. The government of July, following a similar course for a time, established independent banks at Lyons, Marseilles, Lille, Havre, Toulouse and Orleans, and also authorized the Bank of France to open branches in fifteen other provincial towns and cities, with the monopoly of issue for every place in which a branch was established. Vigorously pursued, this mixed system of branches and of independent banks might easily have been made the means of introducing banking facilities throughout the kingdom, to the great advantage of the country, which has never ceased to suffer from the backwardness of its development in this respect. But no strong policy was adopted; the government established new banks for a time with reluctance and under hard conditions, and after 1838 withheld its

---

* *Moniteur*, 28 May, 1808.

encouragement altogether; and the Bank of France, opening its branches fitfully and with little regard for public needs, seemed to prefer that affairs should drift.

The revolution of 1848 found in existence, then, the Bank of France with its fifteen branches, and nine independent banks of issue. No system of exchanges or of redemption at a common centre had been adopted by the latter; even the branches of the great Bank redeemed each other's notes only at pleasure; so that France felt all the inconveniences of having many issues of notes with but local credit. The suspension of specie payment and the legal tender power given to the notes of the Bank of France, and to those of the independent banks alike,* added to the confusion, and in the spring of 1848 the provincial government finally cut the knot, by making all the independent banks, branches of the Bank of France. Their shareholders, in exchange for their old stock received shares in the Bank, and the capital of the latter was thus raised to 91,250,000 francs.† This practically reestablished the monopoly in the form in which it had been projected by Napoleon, and although a vigorous discussion of the advantages of freedom in banking has been carried on in France, all subsequent legislation has tended to strengthen the existing system. The government of Napoleon III. urged the extension of its branches by the Bank, and in 1857 even called for the establishment of one in every department within ten years. The Bank was reluctant, but before 1869 sixty-five branches had been authorized. The republican government in 1873 again applied the spur, and in 1880 all the required branches had been authorized, although a few were not brought into operation until as late as 1882.

3. After all, however, it would seem that the branches thus established can fill but imperfectly the place of local banks.

---

* *Moniteur*, March 16 and 26, 1848.
† *Moniteur*, April 29, 1848.

A branch of the Bank of France has a capital allotted to it by the Bank and is then required to carry on its business strictly under the supervision of the latter, and without engaging in any operation with other branches, except by special leave, so that its business, even to the rate of discount, is directed by a policy settled at Paris and not with reference to local wants. It has a board of directors selected by the governor of the Bank, from a list of candidates in some cases made up at Paris and in some by local stockholders, where the latter represent half of the capital allotted to the new branch. The real authority, however, is exercised by a manager appointed by the government, frequently a stranger, and assisted by subordinates sent from the capital. That under such circumstances, more than one-half of the discounts of commercial paper made by the Bank should be made at its branches, as has been the case ever since 1848, is better evidence of the great demand for banking facilities in the provincial towns, than of the success of the present organization in answering this demand.

That the want of such aid from independent banks as a freer system would have given has been seriously felt by the country, appears clear from the measures to which the French government has found itself driven in two periods of political revolution. It has been remarked that from 1814 for many years the Bank of France was the bank of the bankers rather than of the merchants.* The position of intermediary between the bank and the great class of borrowers on a small scale, should have been held by a class of independent banks; it appears, in fact, to have been held by private bankers, and during the revulsion which accompanied the revolution of July, 1830, this class of establishments either disappeared or became inactive, so that a part of the usual machinery of commerce, never adequate, was for a time absolutely wanting, and it seemed impossible for the normal movement to begin again. The

---

* Courtois, *Histoire* p. 156.

THE BANK OF FRANCE. 97

Chambers therefore voted that loans should be granted by the government for the relief of commerce to the extent of sixty millions, one-half to be lent directly by a public commission, and the other to be used in establishing public discount-offices in Paris, and in the departments. The loans were made at four per cent. and upon security, and the business would seem to have been managed with better success than could have been expected; for of the thirty millions of direct loans, made to industrial establishments and divided between Paris and the departments with tolerable equality, the amount still unpaid in 1870, and then set down as either bad or doubtful, was only about 900,000 francs. The discount office in Paris discounted paper to the amount of 20,629,000 francs, the securities averaging a little less than 560 francs each, and of this not quite two per cent. was still unpaid in 1841. The operations of the ten or more discount offices opened in the departments are not carefully reported.*

After the revolution of 1848, which carried down the great discount houses in Paris, France was again found to be practically destitute of any banking system which could reach the smaller commercial interests, and the government again found itself compelled to establish in haste the machinery needed for such a crisis.† By a combination of private capital with public, discount offices were established, both in Paris and in the departments, with an organization and powers which made them strongly resemble independent banks, in which the State was a shareholder. In sixty-seven cities of France, including Paris, the operations of these discount offices in 1848, 1849, and 1850 were greater in amount than those of the Bank of France for the same years. A considerable number of these offices

---

* See Courtois, *Histoire*, 138, for a valuable notice of these operations.

† *Moniteur*, March 8, 1848. Courtois, *Histoire*, 178; *Dictionnaire de l'Economie Politique*, art. "Comptoirs d'Escompte."

were allowed to continue their business for several years after the revival of affairs under the Second Empire, and some of them were finally reorganized as banks of discount, repaying to the State its share of the original capital.*

At the present day the state of things is so much changed that it is hardly probable that any crisis of affairs would find such a hiatus in the banking organization as existed in 1830 and 1848. The number of independent banks of discount has finally been greatly increased, and this not merely in the great cities, and the Bank of France, as we have seen, now has a branch in every department. Embarrassment might still be caused in some cases by the provision in the statutes of the Bank which requires three signatures upon all paper discounted by it, unless accompanied by certain specified collaterals, this provision tending to bring in some intermediary party between the actual borrower and the Bank; but the agencies for banking now exist throughout the country, and it would only remain to provide for the details of access to them. But for the monopoly of issue given to the Bank, these agencies would probably have existed long ago and would have reached a much higher development than they have as yet. Deprived of the use of that form of credit which is chiefly in demand in the more remote districts, banking capital has spread itself but slowly, and the privileged institution has found little occasion to exert itself to supply the want, until stimulated by peremptory legislation.

That the Bank of France itself now meets the public wants much more freely than formerly, is clear from the great diminution in the average importance of the securities discounted by it. Before 1830 these securities were on the average not far from 2,500 francs each in amount; from that point they

---

* One of these became the present Comptoir d'Escompte of Paris, a bank having a capital of 80,000,000 francs. Courcelle-Seneuil, *Traité*, 187.

THE BANK OF FRANCE. 99

have fallen irregularly, but still with a marked general tendency, until the average now appears to have settled permanently at less than 900 francs.* As this change has taken place, notwithstanding an immense increase in the aggregate loans of the Bank and a great rise in the scale of financial operations at Paris as well as at other centres of business, we can only conclude that the Bank now systematically admits to its portfolio, in larger proportion than formerly, the paper coming to it directly or indirectly from traders of the smaller class.

4. We have already referred to the suspension of specie payment by the Bank of France in March, 1848. The suspension was authorized, the notes made a legal tender, and the issue of notes of 100 francs permitted, on condition that the issues of the Bank, and of all the independent banks soon after consolidated with it, should not exceed 452,000,000 francs. Political and socialist agitation destroyed all commercial confidence and a rapid liquidation went on; the discounts of the Bank fell off, specie flowed in, and in June specie payment was practically resumed, and the legal tender provision might perhaps have been abrogated with safety, had the bank been left to itself. The Treasury, however, was embarrassed, the Bank saw no other means of using its resources profitably, and advances to a considerable amount were therefore made by it to the government. Partly as a consequence of these relations with the government the limit of the note circulation was raised in December, 1849 to 525,000,000 francs,† and the suspension of specie payment was not ended, and the legal tender power of

---

* Some of the paper discounted by the Bank of France in considerable masses for bankers and others is extraordinarily minute. In 1879. out of 3,902,213 pieces discounted at the Bank in Paris, 7,842 were for 10 francs or less, 392,845 for from 11 to 50 francs, and 623,232 from 51 to 100 francs. *Comptroller's Report*, 1880, 16. And see in the same place for comparison a statement as to the size of loans in several parts of the United States.

† *Moniteur*, 23 December, 1849.

the notes destroyed until June, 1850.* By these means, aided by its own great prudence, the Bank not only passed through the gloomy years from 1848 to 1852 without serious loss, but continued when affairs were at their worst to earn a moderate profit for its stockholders.†

A great expansion of the affairs of the Bank began in 1852. The *coup d'état* had at all events removed political uncertainty, commercial confidence was revived, the discounts and advances made by the Bank to individuals rapidly increased, and in 1853 touched the highest point ever before known. The Crimean war brought no interruption of this rapid growth. The Bank felt its share of the burdens of that period, in the difficulties caused by general financial embarrassments, which forced it to import for its own safety specie to the amount of 800,000,000 francs, at a cost varying from $1\frac{1}{8}$ to $1\frac{1}{2}$ per cent.;‡ but it found its compensation in dividends rising in 1856 to 27 per cent. In view of the general expansion it is not surprising that in 1857 the government determined to double the capital of the Bank, raising it to 182,500,000 francs at which it now stands. It is characteristic, however, of the shifty financial policy of the government of that period, that this increase of capital was used as an opportunity for placing a government loan to which the market happened to be unfavorable. The Bank upon raising its 91,250,000 francs of fresh capital was required to invest 100,000,000 in new three per

---

* *Moniteur*, 15 August, 1850.

† At the end of 1848 the Bank of France held overdue paper amounting to 85,000,000 francs. Of this, 76,000,000 were paid in 1849, and subsequent payments soon reduced the balance so that, it is conjectured, the real loss of the Bank from bad debts during the revolution was not over 500,000 francs, although it charged at the time 4,500,000 to profit and loss. Its dividends during 1848, the worst year, were 75 francs on the share of 1000. Courtois, *Histoire*, 186, *note*.

‡ Courtois, *Histoire*, 222; Tooke, *History of Prices*, VI. 85.

cents., issued for the reduction of the floating debt, which had risen to an awkward amount.* The charter was at the same time extended to 1897, authority was given to issue notes as small as 50 francs, and the government was empowered after 1867 to require the opening of a branch of the Bank in every department. But perhaps the most important of the new features of the charter was the provision made as to the rate of discount. For the greater part of its existence the Bank had striven to maintain the uniform rate of four per cent. The statutes of 1808 had fixed the maximum length of the paper to be admitted to discount at three months, but in periods of difficulty the Bank had sometimes lowered this limit to seventy-five, sixty and even forty-five days. In 1854, however, it definitely adopted the policy of a variable rate of discount, but then found itself hampered by a law passed in 1807, which made six per cent. the limit of legally chargeable interest. The charter of 1857 freed the Bank by special exemption from this restriction, allowing it to charge whatever rate it may find advisable, with the provision, however, that the profits earned by charging a rate above six per cent. shall not be divided but carried to a permanent surplus.†

5. The years from 1857 to 1870, although marked by great changes, both in the political world and the financial, hardly

---

* *Moniteur*, 11 June, 1857. Under this law a share of new stock was given to the holder of a share of old, upon payment of 1100 francs, the par being 1000, and this payment, collected upon 91,250 shares, supplied the 100,000,000 francs required by the government. The stockholders, whose shares were worth 4500 francs June 1, had the satisfaction of seeing their stock after doubling quoted at 3050 on June 29. The three per cents. received by the Bank are not to be sold, and now appear among its resources as "Rentes immobilisées (Loi de 9 Juin, 1857) 100,000,000 fr."

† This surplus, which is set down in the published accounts as "Bénéfices en addition au capital (art. 7, Loi de 9 Juin, 1857)" has stood at 8,002,314 francs since 1874.

witnessed any event in the history of the Bank of France, which needs to be noticed in this sketch.* But with the opening of the Franco-German war in July, 1870, the Bank entered upon the most remarkable period of its existence,—that in which its vicissitudes were most startling and critical, its services to the country most distinguished, and the success of its management most brilliant.

Three weeks before the breaking out of hostilities the Bank of France had in its vaults an amount of cash nearly equal to its notes, and amounting to nearly two-thirds of all its cash liabilities.† The approach of war caused a heavy pressure upon the Bank for loans, and both notes and specie were drawn from it in large amounts, and began to find their way, either

---

* Perhaps an exception should be made of the unexpected claim set up by the Bank of Savoy in 1864, which for a moment seemed to threaten the monopoly of the Bank of France. The Bank of Savoy had by its old statutes the right to issue notes and to establish branches; the treaty of annexation saved all existing rights of corporations in the annexed territory; and on this reasoning it was proposed to raise the capital of the Bank of Savoy from 4,000,000 francs to 40,000,000, to open branches and issue notes. The project was favored by many opponents of the monopoly of note issue, and was formidable enough to lead the Bank of France to make the payment of 4,000,000 francs for the surrender of the asserted rights. For notices of this episode see Courtois, *Histoire*, 245; *Economist*, January 16, 1864.

† The chief movements in the account of the Bank of France, caused by the war, can be seen in the following table, given in millions and tenths:—

	Notes.	Deposits.	Cash.	Disc't Paper.	Public Loans.
1870 June 23	1374.	431.9	1318.5	558.1	
Aug. 11	1583.6	582.2	1028.6	1181.7	
Sept. 8	1745.	441.8	808.	1428.3	
1871 June 29	2213.	524.1	549.8	741.9	1403

June 23 was the day when the cash was at its maximum for 1870; August 11 was the day before the suspension; no account was published from September 8, 1870 to June 29, 1871.

THE BANK OF FRANCE. 103

into private hoards or into foreign hands. Neither the government nor the public could see with patience this dispersion of a stock of specie which, it was felt, might be an important resource in the desperate struggle with Germany, and suspension of payment as a precautionary step thus became probable early in August. Shortly afterward the government resolved upon the adoption of a measure suspending the collection of commercial obligations, and this made the suspension of the Bank a necessity. On the 12th of August, then, four weeks from the beginning of the war, a law was passed, as a government measure and with but one dissenting vote in each house,* authorizing the Bank to refuse payment of its notes in specie, and for the second time in its history making its notes a legal tender for debts public and private. The issue was at the same time limited to 1,800,000,000 francs, and authority was given for the emission of notes as small as 25 francs each. On the next day, August 13th, was passed the first of the measures which postponed all commercial debts for one month and then, by successive extensions of time, until July, 1871, without other burden to the debtor than liability for interest until the final payment.† And finally, on the 14th of August, the limit of issues by the Bank was raised to 2,400,000,000 francs, on the ground that for the Bank to continue its discounts it must have a wider margin than was allowed by the law of the 12th. This completed the series of measures under the authority of which the Bank was administered during the war.

---

* In the Senate the solitary negative vote was given by Michel Chevalier. For the laws noticed in the text see *Journal Officiel*, Aug. 13, 14, 15, 1870.

† Under the operation of this law the Bank of France held suspended paper to the amount of nearly 870,000,000 francs. Of this more than two-thirds was paid in before the expiration of the legal term of indulgence; and of principal and interest less than one per cent. was still unpaid at the end of 1874. Courtois, *Histoire*, 263.

The State had at the outbreak of the war obtained a small advance from the Bank, and called for others soon after the suspension. During the siege the branch of the Bank at Tours became the agency by which considerable advances were made to the provisional government at Tours, while the Bank itself was in like manner aiding the government in Paris. When the war with the Commune succeeded that with Germany, these advances had risen in all to 761,000,000 francs, besides a loan of 210,000,000 francs to the city of Paris. The Bank resisted with great difficulty the efforts of the Commune to use its resources in defence of the city, and for several weeks escape from open pillage, or from demands not to be distinguished from it, seemed hopeless. The prudence of the managers, the devotion of their subordinates, and the steady support of one or two members of the revolutionary body itself, carried the Bank safely through the most dangerous episode of its history, and enabled it once more to give its aid freely to the government.* In July, 1871, the loans thus made to the State amounted in all to 1,425,000,000 francs, and the government now happily found itself in such a position that it could cease drawing from this source.†

6. The brief statement given on p. 102 shows distinctly enough the change which a year of war had wrought in the affairs of the Bank. An enormous loan had been made to the State simultaneously with an increase of discounts for individuals, and this had been effected partly by the sacrifice of cash and partly by an increase of notes, the volume of which now stood nearly 800,000,000 francs above the highest point ever

---

* For minute details of the history of the Bank under the Commune, and of the means by which it was saved, see Du Camp, *Les Convulsions de Paris*, III. ch. ii.

† In the *Bulletin de Statistique et de Législation Comparée* for April and May, 1880, is a careful report upon these loans and upon their subsequent payment.

before reached. This increase of notes had been managed with great caution, so that while it necessarily expelled from circulation a considerable amount of specie, it had nevertheless brought about but a slight depreciation of the paper;* and with the repayment by the government of the advances made to it by the Bank, the restoration of specie payment promised to be easy. The government, however, was for the time in no condition to undertake the payment of a domestic debt. It had before it the problem of paying to Germany, in the next two or three years, the great indemnity of five thousand millions of francs, to which it was bound by the treaty of peace; it had yet to learn how far its credit would enable it to make this payment by borrowing in the general market, and the most that could be hoped was that it should not have to call upon the Bank for further aid. The latter could not expect, therefore, for several years to come, to extricate the resources which it had lent to the State.

But while the Bank thus saw its resources unavailable for a movement towards specie payments, it was also called upon to increase at once the assistance given by it to commerce. It was of paramount necessity that productive industry should resume its activity without delay, for it was after all in the production of wealth and its proper use that France must find the means of escape from the economic misery caused by the war, and it was the prosperity and thrift of individuals that must support the credit on which the government now relied

---

* During the war quotations were made of exchange on London and occasionally of gold, indicating in one extraordinary case a premium of four per cent. on specie. After restoration of order gold ceased to be quoted, and the price of exchange on London fell to a level of about 1 per cent. premium. See the *Economist* for quotations both in London and in Paris. Leon Say's *Rapport sur le Payement de l'Indemnité de la Guerre* gives a chart showing the rates of exchange in Paris on London from June, 1871, to September, 1873.

in making its settlement with Germany. The Bank therefore took the bold course of rapidly enlarging its discounts and advances to individuals; and to make this possible, in a country where deposit accounts and checks are but little used, it was authorized in December, 1871, to increase its issue of notes to not more than 2,800,000,000 francs,* and in July, 1872, the limit was further extended to 3,200,000,000.† Such an increase of paper with a forced circulation required, as the condition of possible safety from serious depreciation, a further expulsion of specie from use. The smallest notes thus far issued by the Bank were notes for 20 francs authorized by a law of December, 1870; but the law of December, 1871, raising the limit of the total issue of notes, now authorized the issue of notes as low as 5 francs, and thus facilitated the introduction of the bank paper into all the channels of circulation, small as well as great.

With these preparations the great scheme for the simultaneous payment of Germany and revival of France was carried through. The government borrowed in all the markets of Europe, including that of Germany, but called upon the Bank of France for nothing more than two or three temporary advances, not large in amount and soon repaid. The Bank doubled its discounts of commercial paper for the next three years, and for this purpose increased the note circulation until at its maximum at the end of October, 1873, it nearly reached 3,072,000,000 francs. From the data subsequently published by the Bank it appears that the whole of the increase was made by the issue of notes of not above 100 francs, and the

---

* *Journal Officiel, 1871,* p. 5373.

† *Journal Officiel, 1872,* p. 4970. The provision is contained in Article 4 of the law for a national loan of three milliards, and declares that "le chiffre des émissions des billets.... est élevé provisoirement à trois milliards deux cents millions."

THE BANK OF FRANCE. 107

greater part of it by means of notes of 50 francs and less.* The risks of the operation were amply compensated by its gains. Although the government, in view of the valuable privilege enjoyed by the Bank of making a great issue of notes without the obligation of payment, reduced to one per cent. the interest on its debt to the Bank, the profits from the immense increase of discounts were heavy. A dividend of 20 per cent. for the second half of 1871, 32 per cent. for 1872, and 35 per cent. for 1873 amply justified the conduct of the management in the eyes of stockholders, and once more proved that in periods of suspension no trade flourishes like that of the dealers in credit.

7. The government was able in 1872 to begin its payment to the Bank at the rate of 200,000,000 francs per year; the payment of the indemnity to Germany was completed in August, 1873, and in 1874 the Bank began its preparations for the resumption of specie payments. France having a less expanded state of credit than most other commercial countries had felt the revulsion of 1873 but little, and it was, therefore, possible to make a large reduction in the discounts of the Bank, and thus to carry on the double operation of accumulating specie and withdrawing notes. The withdrawal of small notes of 25 francs and less was carried on even faster than the general reduction of the circulation, in order to force the introduction of specie into general use and thus to insure the presence of a larger mass of metal in the hands of the public before the Bank should begin its payments. The specie in the Bank reached its highest point in June, 1877, when it stood at 2,281,000,000 francs, showing an accumulation by the Bank alone of over 1,500,000,000 francs in three years and a half. Of this specie, not far from sixty per cent. was gold, it being the policy of the Bank to hold much gold, partly because it alone could answer demands for use in foreign trade, and

---

*Economist for 1872, p. 326; the same for 1874, p. 320.

partly because of the uncertainty which obscured the future value of silver.*

The precise period at which payments should be resumed was determined by the law of August 3, 1875, in which it was provided that when the advances made by the Bank to the State should have been reduced to 300,000,000 francs, payment of the notes in specie should begin.† By the end of 1876 only 38,000,000 francs remained unpaid and it would not have been difficult at any time in 1877 to complete the operation. The year was permitted to pass, however, without taking the final step, the Bank in the meantime dealing upon the specie basis. A payment of 10,000,000 francs, which lowered the government debt to the required point, was at last made *pro forma* December 31, 1877,‡ and specie payment was resumed with the opening of the new year, without shock and without much thought on the part of the public. By the terms of the law the notes continued to be a legal tender for all debts, as they are to-day; their forced circulation by non-payment was at an end. It is also to be observed that as the law for resumption did not disturb the previous legislation which had fixed the limit of note circulation for the Bank at 3,200,000,000 francs,

---

* It has often been said that at this time the great nations were "grasping for gold," in a momentary panic caused by the introduction of the gold standard in Germany. See *e. g.* Sherman, *Speeches*, p. 528. A little examination will show, however, that the great demands for gold by Germany, France, and the United States came in succession and not simultaneously and were met without disturbance. While the French accumulation was going on in the years 1874 to 1877 inclusive, that sensitive barometer, the Bank of England rate, averaged 3½ per cent. During the four years it rose but once as high as 6, and then for only 38 days, and was above 4 for only 124 days altogether. These low rates are not observed when nations are "grasping" for specie.

† See Article 28 of the Budget for 1876, in *Journal Officiel, 1875*, p. 6866.

‡ The final instalment of the debt was paid March 14, 1879.

the Bank of France for the first time in its history has the function, when paying in specie, of issuing a legal tender paper of limited quantity.

At the moment of resumption the notes of the Bank remaining in circulation amounted to nearly 2,462,000,000, of francs. This was a heavy reduction from the maximum reached in 1873, but it was still nearly double the usual circulation for the years before the war. The free choice between specie and paper after resumption led to but little diminution of the issues, so that as the result France may be said to have adopted a permanently larger paper circulation. In part this is no doubt due to a considerable expansion of affairs, calling for an ampler circulating medium; but in still greater part it is no doubt the effect of a change of habit generally produced by any protracted use of forced paper,—a change which makes it highly improbable that any nation after such an experience will easily return to the use of paper and coin in the same proportions which it once found satisfactory.

CHAPTER VIII.

THE REICHSBANK OF GERMANY.

1. WHEN the present German empire was established in 1871, the reform of the legislation upon currency and banking was felt to be a pressing necessity. In coinage some German States had ranged themselves under the thaler system and others under the gulden, and in all there was a mass of old coin in circulation of obsolete denominations. The silver standard had been adhered to by all. All the members of the old confederation, except the cities Hamburg, Lubec, and Bremen, and the principality of Lippe, were issuing paper currency for the supply of their own wants. And finally thirty-three banks of issue, with capitals ranging from 1,200,000 marks to 35,000,000, had been established, each upon such basis as the State or city establishing it found good, some holding perpetual charters, some incorporated for terms of years, and some holding only revocable rights. These banks differed materially as to the limit of their authorized issues, and were under different obligations as to the holding of reserve. To reduce this mass of confusion to order and to establish unity of system in currency and banking, was a problem which constantly taxed the German mind for the first four or five years of the new empire.

The law of December, 1871, provided for unity of coinage and prepared the way for the subsequent introduction of the gold standard by the act of July, 1873.* Another law of April, 1874, provided for the extinction of the paper currency issued by the several German States, by creating a currency of imperial treasury notes (reichs-kassenscheine), convertible into gold upon demand at the Treasury, but not a legal tender, and authorizing the distribution of it by loan to the several States, to be used in taking up their local issues of notes.† Of the imperial paper 120,000,000 marks were distributed to the states in the ratio of population, and 55,000,000 more in amounts as required, and by this means twenty local issues, amounting in the aggregate to rather more than 180,000,000 marks, were extinguished. And finally by a law of March, 1875, the banks of issue were brought under a common system and the reform may be said to have been completed.‡

2. The new system required the establishment of a central bank, to be under the immediate supervision and direction of the imperial government, and the subjection of all other banks of issue to a uniform set of regulations and also to imperial supervision. To secure the first of these two objects, advan-

---

* The coinage laws of 1871 and 1873 are to be found, with copious annotations by Soetbeer, in Bezold's *Gesetzgebung des Deutschen Reichs*, Th. II. Band i., this part of the volume being also issued separately as Soetbeer's *Deutsche Münz Verfassung*. See pages 35, 67. For a translation see Laughlin, *Bimetallism in the United States*, 237.

The German law of July, 1873, is often spoken of as a law "demonetizing" silver. In fact it provided for coining gold money and substituting this for silver, but it did not demonetize the silver remaining in circulation, nor has this step ever been taken by Germany, although the government has been empowered to take it when the mass of silver afloat shall have been sufficiently reduced.

† See Bezold, as above, p. 181.

‡ The bank law 1875 is to of be found with Soetbeer's annotations in Bezold, *Gesetzgebung*, Th. II. Band i., 255.

A translation is to be found in the *Statistical Journal* for 1875, 267.

tage was taken of the peculiar position of the Bank of Prussia. Originally established as a government bank, with a capital of 2,000,000 thalers supplied by the State, this bank had been enlarged by the admission of private stockholders until its capital had risen to 20,000,000 thalers, but without the surrender by the State of its power of control or of its disproportionate share of the profits. As a part of the new system the Bank of Prussia now became the Bank of the Empire (Reichsbank); the capital and share of surplus belonging to the Prussian government were paid over, together with 15,000,000 marks for the good will of the establishment; and the capital was then raised by subscription to 120,000,000 marks, the whole of which was thus placed in private hands. The imperial government reserved to itself a direct power of control through the imperial chancellor and also by the appointment of the board of direction, giving to the shareholders the election of a committee charged with certain duties of consultation. The Bank was required to receive and make payments, and to conduct other financial operations for the Imperial Treasury, without compensation, and also to manage free of cost the receipts and payments of the several States of the Empire. It was thus made in everything except its ownership a national bank on a large scale, although not the largest, and had its privileges secured to it for fifty years.

Certain general regulations adapted the thirty-two existing independent* banks of issue to the new system. The exclusive right of issuing banknotes was then given to them and to the Reichsbank, with a provision for transferring to the latter any right of issue which might be surrendered by any of the others. No limit was fixed for the aggregate circulation, but it was required that for all notes issued in excess of 385,000,000

---

* The banks which are here called "independent" are often designated as "private banks," to distinguish them from the Reichsbank. But as they are incorporated, the term "independent" appears less likely to be equivocal for American readers.

marks cash must be held, under the penalty of a tax at the rate of five per cent. per annum for all notes thus issued without such protection, the banks being allowed to count as cash for this purpose German coin, gold bullion and foreign gold, imperial treasury notes, and notes of other banks. It was also required that the cash held, exclusive of the notes of other banks, should in any case be equal to at least one-third of the total circulation, and that the other two-thirds should be protected by discounted paper, having not more than three months to run. The amount of the total issue to be protected by discounted paper instead of cash, or as it is usually called the "uncovered" issue, was also apportioned among the banks, having due regard to the amount of the notes previously issued by each, and to their probable needs in the future,* so that the provisions as to the cash to be held, which we have stated as made for the banks in the aggregate, are in fact applied to each bank by itself. Under this arrangement the limit of uncovered issue allowed to the Reichsbank was originally 250,000,000 out of the 385,000,000 marks. Fifteen other banks, however, declined to issue notes under the conditions required by the law, and the transfer of their rights of issue to the Reichsbank therefore raised its uncovered limit to 273,875,000 marks, as it now stands; the remaining seventeen banks also issuing notes have then a limit of uncovered issues amounting in all to 111,125,000 marks.†

---

* As to this apportionment see Soetbeer's *Bank Verfassung*, in Bezold, as above, 273.

† The account of the Reichsbank for December 31, 1883, shows that the outstanding notes then amounted to 842.5 million marks, and the cash, to 592 millions. As the uncovered limit was 273.9 millions, it follows that the Bank could still increase its issue by 23.4 million marks, without being required to add to its cash. In other words the Bank had a disposable margin of 23.4 million marks which could be paid out either in gold or in notes calling for gold. This margin, it will be seen, bears a close analogy to the banking reserve of the Bank of England.

The notes issued under this system rest upon a solid basis of specie, but in addition, the presence of an ample specie circulation in the country is secured by a provision prohibiting the issue of any notes of lower denomination than 100 marks.

3. In this system are easily traceable the general outlines of the English Bank Charter Act of 1844. The suggested absorption of the entire right of issue by the Reichsbank, emphasized as it is by a provision that the government upon giving due notice may withdraw the right from any bank in 1891, or at the end of any decade thereafter, the fixed limit of notes to be issued without bullion, and the automatic arrangement for the issue of notes against cash above that limit, all are closely copied from the English model. The requirement that the cash shall amount in any case to one-third of the notes is new, and so is the virtual permission to increase the uncovered issue beyond the limit, subject to payment of the tax of five per cent., the last being intended to give a certain degree of elasticity at that point where, under the English law, the rigidity of the line drawn by Peel's Act has sometimes presented a frightful dilemma. This elastic limit has several times taken effect in the case of the smaller banks, but never in the case of the Reichsbank until in December, 1881, and again in September and October, 1882, and in December, 1884, when the issues of the Bank were to a small amount beyond the fixed limit. On these occasions it seems certain that the operation of the elastic provision was successful in saving the German community from what would have a severe spasm of contraction under the usual administration of Peel's Act.*

The notes issued upon this plan are not a legal tender, nor are they received at public offices except by virtue of regulations which the government reserves the right of abandoning. Their credit is maintained by their strict convertibility and by the law which makes them everywhere current in payments to

---

* See the *Economist*, 1882, pp. 41, 1331.

THE REICHSBANK OF GERMANY. 115

any bank of issue. Every bank is required to pay its own notes on presentation; the Reichsbank also, under ordinary circumstances, pays its notes at its branches; and every independent bank is required to redeem its notes at an agency in Berlin or in Frankfort, as the government may determine, in addition to redeeming at its own counter. Every bank of issue is also required to receive at par in payment the notes of every other bank, with the provision that all notes thus received, except those of the Reichsbank, must be either presented for redemption, or used in payments made to the issuing bank or in the city where it is established. This provision, which imposes a safe restraint upon the smaller banks, is also significant from its tendency to allow the Reichsbank alone to obtain anything resembling a national circulation.

4. The leading position of the Reichsbank is indeed well assured by its 220 branches of different grades, which carry on its operations into every part of the Empire, and now far outnumber all the independent banks of issue and their branches. Of the total capital and surplus of the banks of issue the Reichsbank has not less than forty-five per cent.; or if we include all the banks which issued notes down to 1875, it has thirty per cent. of the whole. It issues, however, nearly four-fifths of the entire note circulation, and in a country where the use of deposit accounts is so little developed as in Germany, this fact alone shows that it absorbs a large part of the banking business of the country. Of such use of deposit accounts as exists, however, the Reichsbank has also a large share, in acquiring which its great net work of branches is no doubt of great service. It appears, indeed, to have suffered a large part of its business of holding deposits payable after notice to lapse, and to have developed actively its accounts current, three-fourths of which are kept by its branches. Few of the independent banks have effected any such complete transformation. The Frankfort Bank has even diminished its accounts current

heavily within a few years, while the Bremen Bank holds nearly all of its deposits subject to notice. After all, the note circulation of the German banks of issue, including the Reichsbank, is five times as important as their accounts current.

The chief part of the investments made by the German banks, aside from their heavy reserve of specie, is in the form of discounts, which amount on the average to between two and three times their capital and surplus. They are authorized to lend upon the deposit of securities, merchandise and bullion, and all of these forms of loan appear to be in practice.* The total amount, however, of the loans upon pledge (*Lombardgeschaeft*) is not so great as one-fifth of the loans by discount, and the proportion in which this total is divided between securities, merchandise and bullion does not appear in the published accounts.

Of the net profits of every bank, the law now requires that from so much as is earned in excess of a dividend of four and a half per cent., at least one-fifth shall be annually added to the surplus, until this amounts to one-fourth of the capital. But of the profits of the Reichsbank remaining after this allotment for surplus, it is also provided that an equal division shall be made between the stockholders and the government, with the further cautious provision, that if the dividends of the stockholders are thus raised above eight per cent., the share of the government in the final division shall become three-quarters instead of one-half. Under this provision the government has in some years received from the Bank a revenue of over 2,000,000 marks, the dividends to stockholders since 1875 having varied from five to seven per cent. and a fraction. The dividends of the independent banks vary greatly

---

* Twenty-eight of the branches of the Reichsbank are depots for goods, authorized by the Bank to lend upon the pledge of merchandise.

THE REICHSBANK OF GERMANY.

but do not now often exceed six per cent. The harvest of the German banks was from 1871 to 1875, when the Bank of Prussia, now the Reichsbank, divided from twelve to twenty per cent. annually, and the price of its shares stood between 170 and 250 per cent. The price now ranges in the neighborhood of 135.

NOTE.

In the *Annalen des Deutschen Reichs* for 1875, p. 375, is the balance sheet of the Reichsbank for December 31, 1884. Grouping some of the details for convenience, the account stands as follows, in millions of marks:

Liabilities.		*Resources.*	
Capital	120.	Gold bullion	71.8
Surplus	23.9	German coin	446.
Notes	854.1	Treasury notes	14.3
Accounts current	266.2	Notes of banks	15.4
Profits	4.2	Bills discounted	511.9
Sundries	5.	Loans on security	140.1
		Securities	48.6
		Real estate	19.5
		Sundries	5.8
	1,273.4		1,273.4

It will be observed that according to this account the notes exceeded the cash on hand by 306.6 millions. As the uncovered issue allowed by the law is not quite 273.6, it follows that the Bank had issued notes in excess of the prescribed limit by about 33 millions for the last week of 1884. This probably accounts for the appearance, among the sundry liabilities in the original, of 34,040 marks due under the 5 per cent. note tax.

CHAPTERS.

		PAGE.
I.	DISCOUNT, DEPOSIT AND ISSUE	5
II.	BANKING OPERATIONS AND ACCOUNTS	13
III.	THE CHECK SYSTEM	27
IV.	BANKNOTES	39
V.	THE NATIONAL BANKS OF THE UNITED STATES	48
VI.	THE BANK OF ENGLAND	64
VII.	THE BANK OF FRANCE	90
VIII.	THE REICHSBANK OF GERMANY	110

www.ingramcontent.com/pod-product-compliance
Lightning Source LLC
Chambersburg PA
CBHW020131170426
43199CB00010B/718